Q
IN THE
GARDEN
OF
GRAMMAR

'In Amal Fabian's delightfully inventive tale, grammar isn't just learned—it's lived. Young Q finds himself in the Garden of Grammar, where talking trees and bookworms teach the rules of language with charm and mischief, and energy is made from articles. Drawing on the magical etymology of "grammar" (yes, it shares roots with "glamour"), this story turns punctuation into power and syntax into adventure. A treat for curious children and word-loving adults alike, it's a journey through language that sparkles with imagination, wit and wonder.'

—Shashi Tharoor

Q

IN THE GARDEN OF GRAMMAR

LEARN GRAMMAR THROUGH THIS AMAZING STORY!

AMAL FABIAN

KONARK

Konark Publishers Pvt. Ltd
206, First Floor
Peacock Lane, Shahpur Jat
New Delhi - 110 049
+91-11-4105 5065
india@konarkpublishers.com, us@konarkpublishers.com
www.konarkpublishers.com

ISBN: 978-81-987405-8-8

Edited by Preeta Priyamvada
Cover design and illustrations by Sunayana Nair Kanjilal
Typeset by Saanvi Graphics, Noida
Printed and bound in India by Thomson Press India Ltd

Contents

This book is dedicated to the grammarian inside all of us.

Dear Reader

Thanks for letting this book find you! Grammar is important. It gives us a framework to communicate our thoughts, ideas, and emotions. Without grammar, our sentences would not make much sense. Try using incorrect prepositions and mixing up tenses in sentences, and you'll see what I mean.

This is a story about Q who lives in Alphabet Village. He goes on a journey across the Grammar Dimension visiting magical places such as Articles Station, Punctuation Grove, and Garden of Grammar. He meets and has conversations with people, trees, and a lazy bookworm called Wow. Through these conversations Q learns basic grammar.

The Grammar Dimension is large and there are lots of places to visit. So, take your time when it comes to learning grammar. You cannot learn everything in one go.

This book is not only about grammar. As Q travels through the Dimension, anti-grammatical forces are planning to take over the Garden of Grammar. If that happens, it will lead to days of darkness. It is up to Q, who doesn't know much about grammar, to save his world. Will he succeed? You'll find out.

This book follows the rules of British English grammar.

If you are curious about some aspects of grammar and you want to dig deeper, see the list of grammar resources I've added at the end of the book.

I wish you an adventure with Q in the Grammar Dimension!

Amal Fabian

Acknowledgements

A special thank you to Manoj Mohan for reviewing the grammar. I thank: Vineeta Christine Chandeker for her insightful comments; Steven Baker, my first creative writing teacher; my students from whom I got the idea to write such a book in the first place; and the British Council where I practised the craft of language teaching.

Without the unwavering support of my mother, Usha Fabian, and father, KP Fabian, this book would not have come into being. My sister, Anupa Fabian, and brother-in-law, Vikram D'Mello, have been a formidable editorial team.

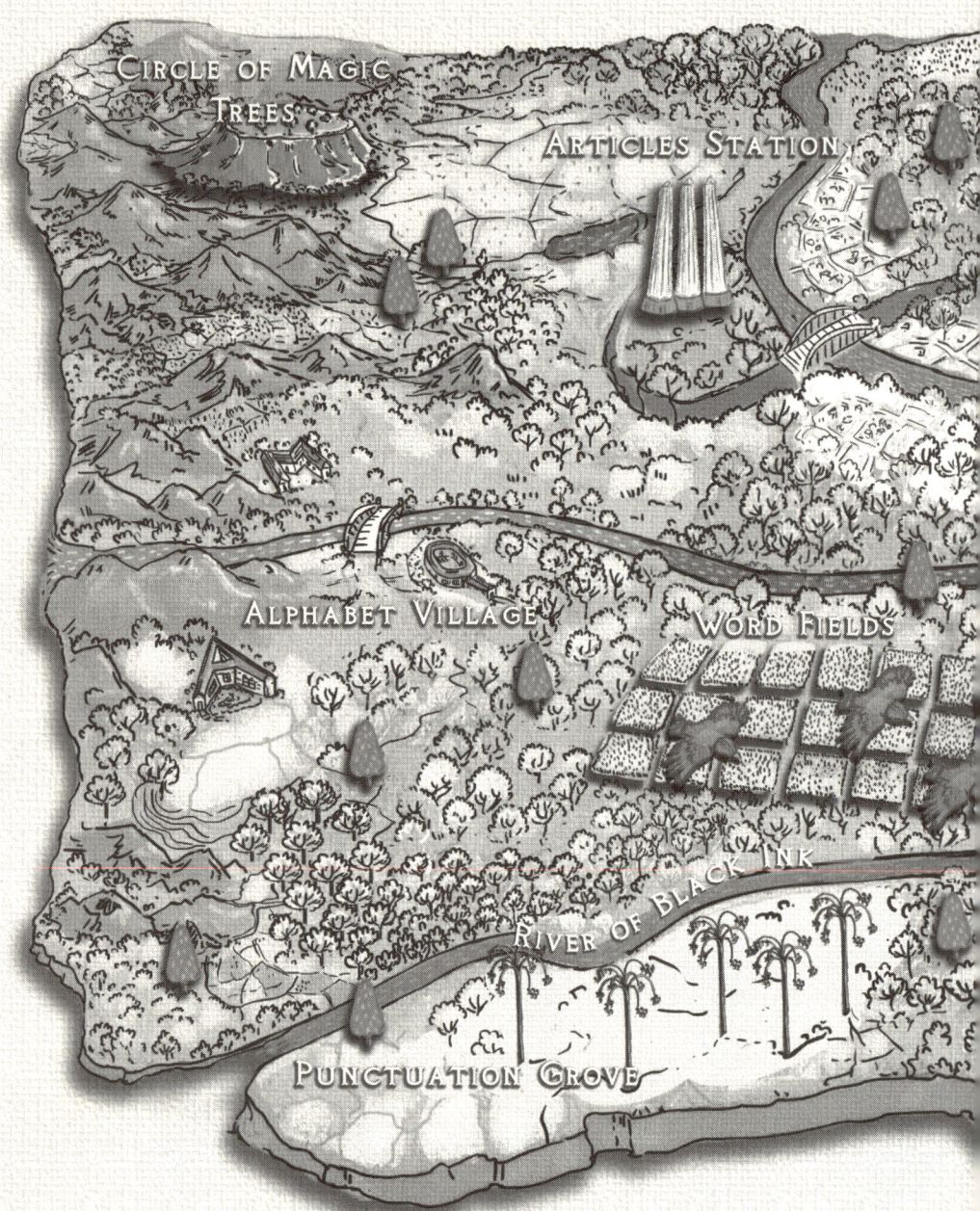

THE GRAMMAR DIMENSION

CIRCLE OF MAGIC TREES

ARTICLES STATION

ALPHABET VILLAGE

WORD FIELDS

RIVER OF BLACK INK

PUNCTUATION GROVE

OCEAN OF INK

CHAPTER 1

The Articles Station

Not far from Alphabet Village, just north of the River of Blue Ink, far away from the Garden of Grammar, P was at home, reading a newspaper.

'Grammar is over-rated. We can communicate without it. Who needs grammar anyway?' P mumbled.

X, his wife, dropped the orange teacup she was holding. It shattered into pieces.

She asked, pronouncing each word clearly, 'What did you just say?'

X raised her left eyebrow as she finished her sentence.

P replied, 'It wasn't me darling. It's here, in today's newspaper. Someone called Q has written an article on why grammar is unnecessary.'

X carefully picked up the broken pieces of crockery from the floor and placed them in a basket. She wondered whether she could glue the pieces together.

She placed the basket on the table and looked straight at her husband.

'Find this person. Show him the Grammar Dimension. Let him see the importance of grammar for himself,' she said.

X raised her left eyebrow when stressing the words *find, show, importance,* and *himself.*

P sighed. This was his first day of retirement. He wanted to catch up on some reading. He had even borrowed three books from the local library.

'Where does he live?' asked X.

'This article says that Q lives in Alphabet Village.'

'You absolutely must go.'

He never could refuse his wife. They had been married for a long time. They had met while they were at grammar school in the town of Biblios. He was good at grammar, but she was excellent at it. X was always top of the class.

Before he left, she whispered something to him.

'Are you sure?' asked P.

'It is a possibility.'

While P was walking towards the village, he thought about the article he had read. *How could Q write such a thing? Does he even know what grammar means to us? I mean the very idea of doing away with grammar. Where would we get energy from? How would we communicate? How would we even survive?*

'Why the long face?' asked a voice.

P scanned the tall trees around him. He saw something brown moving behind the green leaves. A spell-checker owl hopped on to a lower branch.

Spell-checker owls are intelligent birds. They spend most of their time reading books. These birds are also very good at editing sentences. And of course, they can spell any word ever spoken. Spell-checker owls are not allowed to take part in spelling bee competitions.

'Ah, it's you. Yes, well, some fool has written an article saying that grammar is useless,' said P.

'Hoo! Hoo! You have to find him, and show him otherwise,' said the spell-checker owl. It then asked, 'Haven't you retired?'

The owl's brown belly went up and down as it laughed. It was waving its wings and was laughing so much that it almost lost its balance. 'Hoo, hoo, hoo!'

'I'm happy you find my retirement amusing,' said P, 'I must be off.'

There were twenty-six houses in Alphabet Village. Each house was surrounded by a green lawn. A stone bridge crossed a river of dark blue ink. A few children were on the bridge. They were throwing pebbles into the flowing ink.

P headed straight to a house which was by the side of the river. The house was circular, but for a rectangular strip that jutted out onto the lawn. The door was at the end of this strip. P rang the bell.

Opening the door, a man said, 'Good morning, sir. How may I help you?'

P said, 'I need to see Q. Immediately.'

The man brushed away some strands of curly hair that had fallen over his eyes.

'Ooh… Then you should follow me.'

They went down a corridor into the study. P surveyed the room. Its two long walls were curved. A large painting was on one of the curved walls. The painting was a map of the Grammar Dimension: it showed all the important places. P recognised the Punctuation Grove. He could identify the three towers which represented the Articles Station. *Well, the towers don't look exactly like that: they are much thinner. And the Punctuation Grove is not so far north. It's much more towards the south.*

'Beautiful painting of the Dimension. Not accurate, but beautiful,' said P.

'I painted it myself. Eh... Why are you here?'

P nodded while looking at another place in the Dimension—the Word Fields.

'I need to speak with Q. Immediately.'

'Well, here I am. I am Q.'

'You do not look like a troublemaker! Hmm... Did you or did you not write an article saying that we do not need grammar?'

'I'm not against grammar. I just feel that it is... well... not as important as people make it out to be,' replied Q.

'Not important! We live in the Grammar Dimension. Grammar gives us everything. How can it be over-rated?'

'Well... I mean, think about it. I can use words without grammar and still be understood. For example, I can say: "*Long time no see….*" You still understand what I'm trying to say. I can ask you a question. "*Thirsty?*" It's not grammatically correct, but you still understand what I mean. I am asking you a question: *Are you thirsty?*'

'Enough,' said P, raising a hand.

X was right. I will have to show him how important grammar is to us. There is no other way.

On the table, there was a painting of Q and a lady dressed in white. She was holding a book titled: Just Married!

'Where is your wife?' P asked.

'She's gone to organise a book club meeting.'

'When is she coming back?'

'Tomorrow morning. They'll be listening to ghost stories all night long in the forest. I'm a bit scared of….'

P grinned. His wife was a bookworm as well. And she was always organizing book-reading sessions.

He said, 'Would you like to see the Dimension for yourself? Only a few get this chance. What do you say?'

P then turned to look at the painting. His eyes fell on four grammatica flowers. These flowers marked an important place—the

Garden of Grammar. This was the only part of the Dimension he had never been to.

Q had only heard stories about fantastic places outside his village. He was convinced that many of these stories were not real.

'I am ready.'

He scribbled a note for his wife: *Gone to explore the Dimension—Q.* He placed the note under an empty glass.

'Where are my manners?' asked Q, 'Would you like some ink, Mr...?'

'Just call me P... I wouldn't mind some ink.'

'We have red, blue, and green ink.'

'Blue is fine for me.'

Q returned from the kitchen with a glass of cool, blue ink.

'By the way, what do you do?' asked Q.

P finished his ink in one long gulp and smacked his lips.

'I've retired. I used to be in the service of the Grammar Wizard. I really cannot talk about my assignments. There's a balloon somewhere here.'

'It's near the forest. The balloon belongs to the mayor of Alphabet Village.'

'The mayor is an old friend of mine. He won't mind us borrowing it. Let's go,' said P.

'I'll take some clothes for the journey.'

Q went to his bedroom and opened a closet. He brought out a brown bag. In it, he placed a toothbrush, a jar of toothpaste, a comb, four shirts, three pairs of socks, and two trousers. He thought about placing a notebook into his bag, but he decided not to. He put on a jacket which had more pockets than he could use.

They walked towards the outskirts of the village. Q waved at the children standing on the bridge. They were shouting, 'Q! Q! Q!'

The yellow balloon was tied to four trees. The balloon's basket was quite large: it had standing space for at least six people.

Attached to a side of the basket were two propellers—one large and one small.

'Very well,' said P. 'Jump in.'

As they rose into the sky, Q's eyes, which were naturally big, became even bigger. He saw something that he had never seen before. The place he had lived in all his life, Alphabet Village, was spread out below his feet. He saw the river of ink winding its way through the village and disappearing between the hills.

'The houses… Each one is in the shape of a letter! That one is a *B* and that one is an *A*. And the one over there is an *X*,' said Q.

For the first time, he saw his own house from above.

'I live in a house that is in the shape of a *Q*!'

'You do. A long time ago, the original shape of the letter *Q* was a symbol representing a monkey. That's why the letter has a tail, just like a monkey has. Your neighbour's house is in the shape of an *O*. This shape came from a picture of an eye. Look at that house on the

other side of the river. It's in the shape of the letter M. Its original shape was a zigzag line which represented water. As time went by, these symbols changed shape. They began to represent specific sounds. People forgot what symbols the letters of the alphabet originally stood for,' said P.

A flock of birds, with bright red heads and blue wings, was flying towards them.

'Are they word-peckers?' asked Q.

'Word-peckers. They must be heading to the Word Fields. If you listen carefully, you can hear them sing.'

As the birds got closer to the balloon, Q heard a part of their song:

Give us a word to peck at,

Wrr...Wrr...Wrr...

Give us a phrase to tap at,

Wrr...Wrr...Wrr...

Give us a clause to chip at,

Wrr...Wrr...Wrr...

Q asked, 'Are they flying in the shape of a W?'

'When they're in a group, the W formation is the fastest way for them to fly.'

'Are we going where they're going?'

'We're going somewhere else.'

The balloon's basket swayed back and forth in the wind. The sky changed colours—from blinding red to deep green. Flashes of light burst near the balloon.

Pow! Pow! Pow!

Q placed his palms over his ears.

Pow! Pow!

The land was dusty. There were big rocks everywhere. The balloon landed on a long flat stone. In front of Q, there were three slender pink towers. The base of each tower was as big as the basket of their balloon. The towers became thinner as they rose higher. At the top of each tower, there was a long needle.

A woman approached them from the towers.

'P, my dear friend. How are you? What brings you to the Articles Station?'

She had grey hair which was neatly tied into a bun. It was held together by two pencils. The two pencils crossed each other, making an x.

'I need to show this young man how we collect articles,' replied P, with a wink.

'Well, young man, what do you know about articles?' she asked.

'Articles... We use them before nouns. Articles are, *a*, *an*, and *the*. That's all, I think.'

A green bolt of lightning flashed across the sky. The crackling sound of thunder followed. The woman did not even blink.

She laughed and said, 'Is that all? What would you say if I told you that articles are our main source of energy? Your balloon, your lanterns, and your toaster, all run thanks to the work we do here at the Articles Station.'

'Madam...,' said Q.

'Call me Maz.'

'The towers, Maz. What's going up?'

'The three towers are called: Tower *a*, Tower *an*, and Tower *the*. The atmosphere in this part of the Dimension contains three types of energy bubbles: *a*, *an*, and *the* energy bubbles. The towers collect these energy bubbles from the sky and bring them down to us. Quite simple, actually.'

Maz was enjoying the mystery; she did not get many visitors.

'Follow me,' she said.

They went closer to Tower *a*. Inside the tower, there were two tubes—one was yellow and the other blue. In the yellow tube, words were rising. In the blue tube, sparkling balls of energy were tumbling down.

'What is happening?' asked Q.

'In the yellow tube, all the words which need the article *a* are going up. When the words are at the top of the tower, they attract *a* energy bubbles floating nearby. Once a word attaches itself to an energy bubble, it becomes heavy and falls into the blue tube. All the blue tubes lead to a factory where we separate the word from the energy bubble,' Maz explained.

'And this is how we get our energy,' said Q, scratching the top of his head.

'Which words use the article *an*?'

'Well, words that begin with a vowel.'

'Actually, we use the article *an* with words that begin with a vowel sound. Don't forget it.'

Maz searched for P.

She said, 'He must be near the balloon. It can attract lightning. I must warn him. I want you to stay here to manage all the towers. If a tower turns orange, it needs more words. The words are here, in this box. You take a word. Slip it into the tower's opening. The word rises. It attaches itself to an energy bubble. Make sure you put the right word in the right tower. Got it?'

The opening in the tower was a rectangular slit, like the one in a postbox, except this one was much larger.

Q said, 'You must be joking. I'm not ready for this.'

'I never joke.'

Without saying another word, she turned on her heel and left. Q, wringing his hands, watched the towers. All the towers were pink. For a while, nothing happened. Suddenly, one tower turned orange. It was Tower *a*.

'This can't be happening to me,' he muttered.

He shuffled to the box. It was full of words. One of the words was *balloon*. He held the word in his hands. It was warm. He placed the word *balloon* in Tower *a*. The word gently bumped along the sides of the tube as it floated up.

Searching for another word, he found the word *stone*. He dropped it. It fell on his left big toe.

'Ouch!'

This word was a heavy one. He picked it up and placed it in Tower *a*. The word shot up, like a cannonball. Tower *a* was pink again.

He went to the second tower that was now orange. It was Tower *an*. Q peered into the box, searching for a word which began with a vowel. He found the word *elephant*. He placed the word in Tower *an*. The word moved up steadily. Tower *an* was pink again.

He glanced at Tower *the*. It was the only tower he had not been to.

'Every word should go with *the*,' he said to himself.

Three flashes of blue lightning ripped across the sky. Tower *the* turned orange. Q held two words: *mouse* and *cat*. He placed them in the tower. The word *mouse* chased the word *cat* into the violent sky.

Q was feeling confident; all towers were pink. A splash of green colour appeared over the towers. As it expanded, he imagined that someone was pouring green ink over a blue dome. The sky changed from blue to green.

At the top of the towers, there were small bursts of light. The articles and words were joining. Pow! Pow! It was magic.

Tower *a* turned orange. He found a word: *hour*. He placed it in the tower. The word floated up. It came down a bit before floating up again.

Tower *an* turned bright orange. He searched for a word beginning with a vowel. Q held the word *university*. It was a long word. He clutched it from both ends. And with some difficulty, he placed it in Tower *an*. The word *university* floated up and stopped for a few seconds. It floated up very slowly.

Q stepped back. He gazed in awe at the towers as they swayed in the wind. He was waiting to see bursts of light. Instead, a deep, mournful sound came from the tops of two towers. Wahhh!

The two towers were crimson. The wailing from the towers grew louder and louder. Fortunately, P and Maz were nearby.

'What have you done?' shouted Maz.

'I just put the word *hour* in Tower *a,* and the word *university* in Tower *an*,' said Q.

Maz looked at Q as if she were going to hit him with a heavy word. Shrugging her shoulders, she turned to P.

'What can we do?' asked P.

'We need to immediately send the correct words up. The towers should return to normal after that.'

P was by the box. With expert eyes, he read the remaining words. He picked out two words—*owl* and *umbrella*.

'Q, use these words for Tower *an*.'

P searched for words he could use for Tower *a*. He found the words: *flower* and *garden*. He slid them into Tower *a*. The two words floated up, side by side.

The towers became pink.

'I... I... had no idea,' said Q.

'I can see that,' said Maz, 'I really thought you knew what is what.

How to use articles is what we learn in the first year of grammar school.'

Q sat on the stony ground, staring at the needle of a tower.

'What you need is a notebook. Do you have one?' asked P.

'No,' Q replied.

'She'll give you one. I want you to write down everything you learn during our journey,' said P.

Maz had two pencils in her hair. She slid one out.

'This is a pencil given to me by the Grammar Wizard herself. You will never need to sharpen it.'

She gave Q a notebook, which had yellow pages.

'Thank you,' said Q.

He wrote in spidery handwriting: Articles.

Maz asked, 'How many vowels are there in the alphabet?'

'There are five vowels: *a, e, i, o, u.*'

'When do we use the indefinite article *an*?'

'Before a word that begins with a vowel.'

'If you remember, I told you that we use the article *an* before a word that begins with a vowel sound. For example, we say: *an hour.* Why? Because in the word *hour,* the letter *h* is silent. So, the word *hour* begins with a vowel sound.'

'I have a question. *She is a honest woman.* Is it correct?'

'No, because in the word *honest,* the letter *h* is silent. Just like it is in the word *hour.*'

'She is *an honest* woman.'

'Correct.'

Q made a note of it with his pencil.

Maz said, 'We use the article *a* before words that begin with consonant sounds. Could you give me some examples of consonant letters?'

'K, M, N… mmm… P, Q, R… X, Y.'

'Remember, when you used the word *university* in *Tower an?*'

'That didn't work out well.'

'It is because the word *university* actually starts with a consonant sound. It sounds like the first sound in the word *yum*. So, you should say: *a university*.'

She gave him an encouraging smile which showed all her white teeth.

'Mmm… What you are saying is that I should not only look at the first letter of the word, but also at what the first sound in the word is.'

'Now you are beginning to get it.'

'I have a question. Do I say: *a hill* or *an hill*?'

'You tell me. What is the first sound in *hill*? Is it a vowel sound or a consonant sound?'

'I think it's a consonant sound. So, I would say: *a hill*,' replied Q.

'Correct. You see, in the word *hill*, the letter *h* is pronounced.'

'This isn't so hard.'

'No, it is not. What do you know about the definite article *the*?'

Q wrote four sentences:

The girl is here.
Give me the book.
The sun is in the sky.
The River of Blue Ink is the longest of the four rivers.

After reading the sentences, he said, 'We use the article *the* to talk about something specific or someone specific.'

'Yes, this is after all the *definite* article. What is the difference between these two sentences? *Give me a book. Give me the book.*'

'When you say *'give me a book'*, it can mean any book.'

Maz nodded her head in agreement.

'And when you say *"give me the book"*, you know exactly which book you want me to give you,' said Q.

'Yes. When I say *"give me the book"*, both of us know which book I am talking about. Could you give me the notebook?'

Maz wrote in loopy handwriting: *A girl is here. The girl wants to know more about articles.*

'Are the articles used correctly in these two sentences?' she asked.

'Yes, they are. In the first sentence, we don't know anything about the girl. So, we use the indefinite article *a*. In the second sentence, we know whom we are referring to—the girl who is here. So, we use the definite article *the*.'

'This was the first use of the definite article which I wanted to talk about. There are some other uses of the definite article *the*. We'll speak about two of them. We use the definite article to talk about something that is unique. Look at your sentence: *The sun is in the sky.* We have only one sun. That is why we use the definite article with it. Could you tell me another use of the definite article *the*?'

Q read his last sentence: *The River of Blue Ink is the longest of the four rivers.*

He said, 'We use the article *the* when we want to talk about the longest, or the biggest, or the tallest.'

'Yes. We use the definite article with the superlative form of an adjective.'

Walking up to them, P asked, 'How is the grammar lesson going?'

'Very well... He'll be able to manage the Articles Station from now on,' replied Maz.

Hoping it would not be anytime soon, Q placed his hands in his coat's largest pockets and crossed his fingers.

'Maz, do you know what I would very much like to see?' asked P.

'What might that be?'

'The zero article engine.'

'But it is top secret. How do you know about it?'

'Please show it to us, Maz. I've heard so much about it.'

'Alright, I will. Don't tell a soul. I am not supposed to show it to anyone.'

'Our lips are sealed.'

P moved his index finger across his lips. Maz chuckled as she left.

She returned holding something that looked like a mini-windmill in her hands. She was also carrying a brown paper bag.

'It is experimental.'

Maz laid the mini-windmill on the table. She took out some words from the paper bag. They were much smaller than the ones in the box near the towers.

'Do you know what the zero article is, Q?' she asked, with a twinkle in her eye.

'Nope.'

'The zero article is used when we do not place any article before a noun.'

'Uhhh... Okay.'

'We use the zero article when talking about things in general', she said, 'These words have been made by a team of word-peckers with especially sharp beaks. Could you read the words for us?'

The words were on the palm of her hand.

He said, 'Ehh… Love... Hope... Happiness...'

'Say a sentence with the word *love*.'

'*Love* is all you need.'

'Congratulations! You have just used the zero article. Put these words in the opening.'

'Do I have to?'

'Have courage,' said P.

Q placed the words—one by one—into a tube which was connected to the engine of the mini-windmill.

The four blades spun, making a soft whirring sound.

P said, 'When we use the energy from indefinite and definite articles—*a, an, the*—there is always some smoke that goes into the atmosphere. Some pollution... This engine, on the other hand, uses the zero article, and so gives out no smoke. This means no pollution. That's the beauty of the zero article. It's how we'll get our energy in the future.'

'The zero article is a clean source of energy. We are still perfecting the technology, though. It will take time. The Grammar Council is working on it,' said Maz.

Q wrote: *We use the zero article when we talk about things in general.*

Maz looked over Q's shoulder to check what he was writing.

She said, 'We don't have time to talk about the zero article. Someone will tell you more about it.'

'You've been an excellent teacher,' said P. 'We must be on our way. Your sky is even more unpredictable in the evening.'

'My love to X,' Maz said.

'She always talks about you and all the good work that happens here.'

Maz said to Q, 'Lovely meeting you. I hope you are now comfortable with the use of definite and indefinite articles'.

'I am... And I'm really, really sorry for what I did to the towers.'

'Don't worry young man, these things happen. Always be curious when learning grammar. That's the secret, you know, curiosity.'

'Curiosity. I'll keep it in mind. Thanks.'

'We are all counting on you,' said Maz.

'Counting on me to do what?'

'Q, hurry up and get in. No time for chit chat,' said P.

They flew away from the Articles Station. The sky was now peaceful.

'I never imagined that articles play such an important role in our lives. The Articles Station must be the most amazing place in the entire Dimension,' said Q.

'You think the Articles Station was amazing? Our journey has just begun!'

Stars appeared above them. A powerful current of air carried the balloon north.

CHAPTER 2

The Circle of Magic Trees: The Parts of Speech I

The sun was rising when P and Q reached the mountain. Its top was as flat as a page. On the surface, there were trees. All the eight trees formed a circle: this was the Circle of Magic Trees.

'Those leaves are so large,' said Q.

The rectangular leaves of the trees were of the same size as the A4-size paper we use.

'Walk around. Speak with the trees,' said P.

Q stumbled out of the basket. He took some time to adjust to the thin air, and then he went to a tree. Its branches stretched out in all directions, protecting him from the strong rays of the sun. The tree's ancient roots clutched the ground. Q examined the gnarled trunk.

P shouted, 'You have to talk to the tree!'

'Umm... Hello, my name is Q, from Alphabet Village.'

Nothing happened. Q felt a bit foolish. He looked at a branch. The large beige leaves were still. They were like sheets of handmade paper. Suddenly, the leaves fluttered.

'Weee speak through the breeze. I represent a part of speech. I represent the noun.'

Q shuddered: he had never heard a tree speak before.

'Leave meee... Meet the others.'

'Please tell me something about nouns,' said Q.

'Humpf... Alright... I shall tell you about different types of nouns. There are common nouns and proper nouns. Common nouns are nouns such as: *pen, balloon, word-pecker, teacher, writer,* and *village.* Do you see a pattern?'

'They are general names of things, animals, people, and places. And, what's interesting is that they don't refer to a specific thing, animal, person, or place.'

'Humpf... You are right. Common nouns name a class of things, animals, people, or places. Proper nouns name specific places, persons, or events.'

'For example: *Alphabet Village, Q,* and *Grammar Day,*' said Q.

'You are right. We also have abstract and concrete nouns. Could you tell me the difference between the two?' asked the tree.

'Not really...'

'Humpf... Then you do not knoow much about nouns after all. Abstract nouns are nouns that you cannot knoow through your five senses. You do knoow what the five senses are, don't you?'

'My five senses are: sight, hearing, smell, taste, and touch.'

'Humpf... Yezzz. *Love, hate,* and *hope* are examples of abstract nouns.'

'And so, I guess concrete nouns are nouns that I can know through my five senses. Examples of concrete nouns are *tree, bird,* and *ink.* I can *touch* a tree. I can *hear* a bird chirp. And I can *taste* ink.'

'Yezzz. Give P this message. Tell him the Uncountables wish to speak with him.'

'The Uncountables?'

'You can speak about uncountable nouns with them. Leave meee in peace. Meet the other trees.'

Q met the next tree. It was a tall tree with short, thick branches.

'I stand in for the grumpy tree you just met. I represent pronouns,' said this tree.

'You mean words that stand for a person, such as *I, you,* and *she?*' asked Q.

'Yes, and pronouns can also represent things as well. There are different types of pronouns. Let me start with the pronouns in the nominative case: *I, you, he, she* and *it* are used in the singular form and *we, you,* and *they* in the plural form. Can you give me a sentence with a pronoun in the nominative case?'

'*I* am with the magic trees.'

'Nice. *I* is a pronoun in the nominative case. In the objective case we have—*me, you, him, her, it, us, you* and *them,*' said the tree, '*I gave the book to her.* Here, the pronoun "her" is in the objective case. We cannot say: *I gave the book to she.*'

Q was writing all this down. The tree was silent despite the breeze. It was thinking.

'Do you know all the possessive pronouns?' asked the tree.

Q wrote a list in his notebook and read it out: '*Mine, yours, his, hers, its, ours, yours, theirs.*'

'Whose notebook is that?' asked the tree.

'It's mine.'

'Nice. I'm happy you answered my question with a possessive pronoun. About indefinite pronouns. An indefinite pronoun doesn't refer to a specific thing or person. Can you think of any indefinite pronouns?'

'I can't think of anything.'

'Well, *anything* is an indefinite pronoun. Other indefinite pronouns are—*everything, nobody, anybody, somebody, all,* and *many.*'

The tree representing pronouns was silent again for a while.

'About reflexive pronouns,' said the tree.

'*Myself, yourself, himself, herself, itself,* mmm… *ourselves, yourselves,* and *themselves.*'

'Nice. You have named all the reflexive pronouns. There are two ways to use reflexive pronouns. The first way is to use the reflexive pronoun to reflect back to a noun or a pronoun in a sentence. Here is an example: I gave *myself* a treat today and read some poetry.'

'Do trees read?'

'We do. In the sentence I just said, the one about reading poetry, the reflexive pronoun *myself* reflects back to the pronoun *I.* We use the reflexive pronoun to talk about something that the pronoun or noun does to itself.'

'Okay. I see that.'

'There is another way to use the reflexive pronoun. We also use it to emphasise who performs an action.'

'Example?'

'He *himself* wrote the book.'

'Mmm... Here, you want to emphasise the fact that he wrote the book.'

'Yes. He wrote the book: no one else did,' said the tree.

'Are there any other types of pronouns I should know about?'

'This is not the right time to tell you about relative pronouns. Take one of my twigs. Keep it with you. When the time is right, plant this twig to find out about relative pronouns.'

Q snapped a twig. He unbuttoned his coat and carefully placed the twig in an inner pocket.

The tree said, 'Ooh. Before you go, I must tell you about demonstrative pronouns.'

'I think I know what they are. *This, that, these,* and *those* are demonstrative pronouns.'

'Could you give me a sentence with a demonstrative pronoun?'

Q reached out and touched a leaf.

'*This* is light.'

'You really know your pronouns. Time for you to meet those other trees. Till we meet again. Bye, bye.'

'Bye.'

The next tree was round. It was covered in brown leaves; Q could not see any of its branches.

'I am the adjective tree,' said a high-pitched voice.

'Do you describe nouns?'

'Yes, it is true, quite true. I modify nouns. Without me, nouns would have no life, no colour, no personality. They would be quite boring, indeed.'

'You are an important tree. Is there anything I should know about adjectives?'

'Do you know about the comparative and the superlative forms of adjectives?'

'Oh, yes. I do. Here's an example: *smart, smarter,* and *smartest,*' replied Q.

'Fabulous! And there are adjectives which do not end in *-er* and *-est.*'

'*Beautiful, more beautiful,* and *most beautiful.*'

'Brilliant! And there are adjectives which do not follow the forms we just talked about.'

'I don't know what they are.'

'They are irregular adjectives. What are the comparative and superlative forms for the adjective *good*?' asked the tree.

'Mmm… *good, better,*… mmm… *best*!'

'Yes, in the same way, we have *bad, worse,* and *worst.*'

Q nodded his head while writing the different forms of the irregular adjectives.

'List all the possessive adjectives,' said the tree.

'Well… mmm… First, can you say a sentence with a possessive adjective?'

'*It's my ink pot.*'

'Ahhh… So, *my* is a possessive adjective.'

'What are the other possessive adjectives?'

Q thought about the sentence: *It's my ink pot.* He replaced *my* with the other possessive adjectives: *It's your ink pot. It's his ink pot…*

'The possessive adjectives are *my, your, his, her, our, your,* and *their,*' said Q.

'Do not forget. *Its* can also act as a possessive adjective.'

'There is a word-pecker. And that is *its* ink pot.'

'You are correct. Be careful when you use *its* and when you use *it* apostrophe *s.* How about this? *Its my inkpot.*'

Q asked, 'Is there an apostrophe in your *its*?'

'No.'

Q wrote: *Its my inkpot.* 'It looks right to me,' he said.

'There needs to be an apostrophe there. The possessive adjective *its* shows possession. But there is already a possessive adjective: *my.*'

Q added the apostrophe: *It's my inkpot.* 'I see what you mean. *It is my inkpot.*'

'Did the tree representing nouns tell you about attributive nouns?'

'No.'

'I thought as much. Let us look at this phrase—*grammar* school. The two words, *grammar* and *school,* are nouns. And the word *grammar* is an attributive noun. It modifies the noun *school.*'

'The word *grammar* sounds like an adjective to me.'

'You are right. An attributive noun acts like an adjective,' said the tree.

'Mmm… A noun can function as an adjective.'

'When we started our conversation, I said adjectives modify nouns. This is true. However, there are times when we use adjectives without nouns.'

'Really?'

'If we are talking about a group of people that we can easily identify, we need not have a noun. The adjective acts like a noun. *The rich… The poor… The young…*'

'*The young* are always restless.'

'I agree. Young trees are especially restless. They find it so difficult to be still,' said the tree.

'The Uncountables.'

'Did you just say the Uncountables?'

'Yes. We have to meet them.'

'Then you do not have much time with us.'

'Is there anything else I should keep in mind when using adjectives?'

'Always take your time to choose the right adjective.'

'Breakfast time,' shouted P.

Q walked to P, who was holding a cheese sandwich and a banana. Maz, from the Articles Station, had packed some food for them. They stood in the shadow of the balloon.

'How I wish I had come here when I was in grammar school', said Q, as he peeled his banana.

'It's not easy to bring people here,' said P. 'There are steps carved onto the side of the mountain. It still takes a whole day of climbing to reach the top.'

'When did you come here last?'

'Let me see.... A year ago. The tree representing conjunctions had written a book. I had to collect the pages.'

'How did you do it?'

'There were beautiful sentences on its leaves. The book was about the importance of conjunctions—little words like *and* and *but*. I plucked all the leaves and put them in order.'

'Was it difficult?'

'Not at all. The pages were numbered.'

'What a way to write a book!'

P took a sip of red ink.

'Did the trees tell you anything interesting?'

'Well, I have learnt about nouns, pronouns, and adjectives. Oh yes... The noun tree told me to tell you that the Uncountables want to speak with you.'

'The Uncountables? Now, what would they want to tell me? Hmm... You'd better meet the other trees. We may have to leave sooner than I thought.'

Chapter 3

The Circle of Magic Trees: The Parts of Speech II

Q went to the fourth tree. It had only one low branch, a few branches in the middle, and a few more on the top. There was a lot of space between the middle and top branches.

'I am a magic tree. I represent the verb.'

'The verb.'

'The verb. I'll tell you something while there is still a strong breeze. The verb is the most important part of speech. No doubt about it. After all, without yours truly, nothing can happen. Ever. Nothing at all. All the nouns in a sentence would just sit there twiddling their thumbs with nothing to do.'

'I never thought about it.'

'It would be a good idea for you to start thinking about such things. I'll start with the infinitive. The infinitive is the base form of the verb with *to.'*

'*To crawl... To walk... To fly...*'

'Good. Verbs are divided into two categories. You know what they are, don't you?' asked the tree.

'I don't.'

'The two categories are: *action verbs* and *state verbs*. I'll start with action verbs. *I am talking to you.* The verb in the sentence I just said, *talking*, is an action verb. *Listen, dream, write*—these are all action verbs. Action verbs are all about action—about doing something.'

This tree spoke softly; Q could not hear everything it was saying. He took two steps forward so that he was closer to its trunk. The tree's whispering voice surrounded him.

'State verbs are verbs that describe a state of being.'

Q turned his left ear towards a branch so that he could listen better. He had never heard of state verbs before.

'State verbs normally fall into four categories. The first is mental states. This includes verbs such as *know, think,* and *believe.* Say a sentence with one of these verbs.'

'Sorry, but can you give an example? Please?'

All this talk of state verbs so high above the ground was making Q quite dizzy.

'I *know* a lot about grammar,' said the tree.

'Ahhh... So, *know* is a state verb.'

'Yesss, the verb doesn't describe an action. Now, it's your turn.'

Q went through the list of verbs he had just written.

'I *believe* that the eight parts of speech are wonderful.'

'They truly are... The second category is of emotional states, such as *like, love,* and *hate.*'

'I *love* listening to the spell-checker owls hooting in the evening,' said Q.

'They do sound melodious.'

Q was breathing deeply. He bent down, placing his hands on his knees.

'Have an apple from one of my branches,' said the tree.

He plucked an apple and took a bite. It was the juiciest apple he had ever eaten.

'I'm feeling much better. Thanks.'

'Shall we carry on?'

'Huh.'

'The third category of state verbs relates to the senses. Here are some examples: *see, hear, smell,* and *taste.*'

'This apple *tastes* delicious.'

'I'm thrilled you like it. The fourth category is of possession. This includes verbs such as *own, have,* and *possess.*'

'I *have* a pencil.'

'Yesss.'

Q went over the four categories of state verbs. In his mind, he was making a sentence for each verb.

'When you use a state verb, you can't end it with *ing*,' said the tree.

'I can't?'

'I'll take the state verb *know*. I can't say: I *am knowing* about state verbs. I should say...'

'I *know* about state verbs.'

'That's right. Here is another state verb—*have*. I can't say: I *am having* a pencil. I should say: I *have* a pencil.'

'Mmm… How about this? *I am having a snack.* Isn't this okay?'

'It is. Here, we aren't talking about a state, but about an action. In what you just said, the verb *having* means that you are *eating* a snack. It's an action verb.'

'So, it depends on whether the verb describes an action or a state.'

'Yesss. Listen carefully. Here are two sentences with the verb *think*. *What do you think about grammar? What are you thinking about?*'

'In the first sentence, you want to know what I think about grammar. You want to know what my opinion of grammar is. The verb *think* is a state verb. In the second sentence, the verb *thinking* is an action verb. You want to know what I am thinking about right now.'

'Yesss, yesss. I'm delighted my apple has given you some energy. I'll tell you about gerunds.'

'I know all about them. They are verbs which end in *ing*. They are verbs which act like nouns.'

'Some examples of gerunds?'

'*Swimming, reading, travelling.*'

'Yesss, those words can be gerunds. A gerund is made by taking the *ing* form of the verb. A gerund acts like a noun. Say a sentence with a gerund.'

'My wife enjoys *swimming*.'

'The verb *swimming* acts as a noun.'

'Gerunds are easy.'

'Tell me something about the present participle.'

'I know that present participles are verbs which also end in *ing*. I don't know anything else about them.'

'What you said is right. The present participle is made by taking the *ing* form of the verb. The present participle has many functions. I'll talk about two of them. First, it describes an action in progress. *The sun is shining.*'

'The verb *shining* is an action in progress. I'm listening to you.'

'Second, the present participle modifies the noun. I'll take the verb *laugh*. Its present participle is *laughing*. The *laughing* boy is here.'

'Mmm... Here *laughing* describes the *boy*. The present participle acts like an adjective.'

'It does. Whisper a sentence using a present participle.'

Q thought for a while; his mind was blank.

The tree said, 'The *whispering* tree is talking about verbs.'

'Ah, here, the verb *whispering* is in the present participle. It acts like an adjective.'

'Yesss. Say a sentence with a present participle.'

Q whispered, 'The *singing* word-peckers fly in the sky.'

'That's right.'

'I've learnt so much about verbs.'

'It's time for you to leave my leaves,' said the hushed voice.

Q stood at the edge of the mountain. He saw the tops of many clouds floating by. A small, fluffy blue cloud was near him. Q wished he could snuggle into it and read his favourite novel. The cloud was still for a while, before it speedily drifted away.

CHAPTER 4

The Circle of Magic Trees: The Parts of Speech III

The wind was so strong that Q's curly hair was being blown to one side. With some effort, he walked to the next tree.

'I represent the adverb. Adverbs modify verbs, adjectives, and even other adverbs. I can change the way you walk and how you talk. How about that?'

'But, how?'

'*He walks very quickly.* The adverb *quickly* modifies how he walks. And, the word *very* modifies the adverb *quickly.* The word *very* is also an adverb. When you are with me...'

The wind died down. After a minute or so, a breeze started to blow through the tree.

'Why don't you sit on one of my branches? You'll be more comfortable.'

This tree had six sturdy branches. Q sat on one of them and his legs dangled in the air.

The tree said, 'I'll tell you about six types of adverbs. They are adverbs of manner, adverbs of time, adverbs of place, adverbs of reason, adverbs of degree, and adverbs of frequency. You really should write all this down.'

'I'm not sure I understand all these types of adverbs.'

'Don't worry... You'll have examples for each. Let's begin with adverbs of manner: *fast, angrily, happily.* Did you get that?'

'Yes. I'm writing *fast.*'

'There are adverbs of time such as *now, today,* and *tomorrow.*'

'*Now,* I'm learning about adverbs.'

'*Here, there,* and *everywhere* are adverbs of place. May I continue?'

'Grammar seems to be *everywhere.* Yes, please go on.'

'We have adverbs of reason: *thus, therefore, consequently.*'

'I was daydreaming in grammar school. *Therefore,* I must learn all this now,' mumbled Q.

'Did you say something?'

'Umm... Nothing.'

'We have adverbs of degree: *very, much, little.*'

'I'm learning so *much* about adverbs.'

'The last type are the adverbs of frequency: *once, always, never.*'

'I'll *never* forget this lesson.'

Q checked to see whether his pencil was still sharp. It was as sharp as the tip of a word-pecker's beak.

'That's enough about adverbs for one day. I hope to see you again, soon,' said the tree.

The next tree had two branches which curved upwards. It was in the shape of a vase.

'I represent prepositions. They show the relationship between two words or two phrases. You are *near* me.'

'The word *near* is a preposition,' said Q.

'Oh, yes, it is. There are different types of prepositions. Would you like me to tell you about them?'

'Yes, please.'

'We shall talk about three types of prepositions. First, there are prepositions of location. The word *near* is a preposition of location.'

'Are *above* and *beyond* prepositions of location as well?'

'They are. Shall we talk about the second type of prepositions?'

'Sure.'

'These are the prepositions of direction. Some examples are *towards* and *up*.'

'My wife often says: I am going to the market *via* the library. Is *via* a preposition?'

'It is a preposition of direction.'

'Mmm…'

'The third type are the prepositions of time. For example: *in, at,* and *since*.'

'How are these words prepositions of time?'

'*In* the morning, word-peckers bathe in black ink. *At* night, they sleep in their nests. Word-peckers have been making words in the Word Fields *since* the beginning of grammar.'

'Now, I get it.'

'During our conversation, your balloon left the mountain. By the way, the word *during* is also a preposition of time.'

'I'll be back soon,' P shouted.

The balloon was rising and moving away.

Q sprinted behind the basket of the balloon. He stretched his arms to grab a rope that was hanging from it, but he could not reach it. He tripped on the root of a tree. His nose hit a branch.

'Ouch!' Q yelled.

'Aha! So, you know me already,' said a sing-song voice.

This tree had all its branches on one side except for one that was on the other side. And Q had hit it.

He pinched his nose as the balloon was disappearing into the clouds below. What was he going to do?

'I represent interjections. An interjection is a word that expresses an emotion, such as being surprised or shocked. When you say *aha* or *ouch*, you're using an interjection.'

'Wow!'

'There you go again. *Wow* is my favourite interjection. I know a bookworm named *Wow*. It is always snoozing in books. Ooh…There isn't much time left for you. You should meet the last tree. The breeze won't be here for long. It's a booorring tree, not as much fun as I am. Since you're here, you might as well meet all eight of us.'

Q stood under a tree whose branches were longer and thinner than those of the other trees.

'I am about to describe myself to you, but you are not interested. Hurrrr.'

Q apologised. He said that he was thinking about how long it would take to climb down the mountain.

'Do not worry. P shall return. I am the tree representing conjunctions. Conjunctions connect words, phrases, and clauses.'

'You mean you represent the words *and... but... or.*'

'That is I.'

'But, that's not boring.'

'Hurrr... Who said I am boring? Which tree? Tell me. Tell me right now.'

Its slender branches twisted themselves angrily, as if they were preparing for a fight. The branches creaked as they moved.

'Tree? No tree. I mean... no one,' stuttered Q.

'About conjunctions. There are two types of conjunctions. The words you just said—*and, but, or*—are called co-ordinating conjunctions. This is the first type.'

'Okay.'

'The second type is called subordinating conjunctions. Examples of subordinating conjunctions are *because, although*, and *when.*'

'Please tell me more about subordinating conjunctions.'

'You shall learn about subordinating conjunctions when you visit the Word Fields.'

'How do you know I will be there?'

'We are magic trees; therefore, we know a great number of things. Unfortunately...'

'Say goodbye to the trees. There's trouble down below,' said P.

'I thought you had left me!'

P did not reply.

The rope from the balloon was just above Q's shoulders. He climbed up the rope and clambered into the basket.

CHAPTER 5

Meeting the Uncountables: More about Articles and Nouns

It was blue everywhere. Q could not even see his nose. The balloon was flying through a large cloud.

'Did you enjoy meeting the magic trees?' asked P.

'I did. They told me so much about the parts of speech.'

'Well... Maz already spoke about the two indefinite articles and the definite article. I suppose, I should tell you about the zero article. Do you remember what it is?'

'We use the zero article when we don't use an article before a noun.'

'Yes. Before we talk more about the zero article, tell me what an abstract noun is.'

'An abstract noun is a noun which we can't touch, see, smell, hear, or taste. *Peace, love, imagination.*'

'What are plural count nouns?'

'Mmm... I'm not sure. I guess they're nouns which I can count, and which are in the plural form. *Clouds, trees, balloons.*'

'Those are plural count nouns,' said Q.

'We use the zero article before an abstract noun or before a plural count noun,' said P.

'Well, trees are plural count nouns. So, I can say: I like *trees*.'

'Now, make a sentence with an abstract noun.'

'*Imagination* is all you need.'

'There are times when we use the definite article before abstract nouns and plural count nouns. It's when we want to talk about something specific. I like *the* trees in my village.'

'You're talking about those trees that are in your village, and not about trees in general,' said Q.

'Right. Now you make a sentence.'

'*The imagination* of a child is limitless.'

'Yes. That's a specific kind of imagination: a child's imagination. Well, that's all I have to say about the zero article.'

'Can you tell me something about the Uncountables?'

'You'll find out for yourself. We're about to meet them.'

The balloon was drifting over an empty football field. Q wondered where all the Uncountables were. Searching the nearby forest, P spotted figures among the trees. Soon, people were entering the field.

Q began to count them—one, two, three, four, five... thirty-one, thirty-two, thirty-three....

'If you start counting, you'll never stop. They are uncountable,' said P.

He was right. It was also difficult to count them properly, as they all looked the same. Everyone was wearing a black silk shirt. Everyone had long silky hair tied into a ponytail. And everyone had a neatly trimmed French beard. Q thought they looked quite fashionable.

The balloon landed in the centre of the field. The Uncountables were everywhere. Q could not see a spot of grass. And, they were still streaming out of the forest.

A man, who looked like everyone else, stepped forward.

'P! I am so relieved to see you,' said the Leader of the Uncountables.

'A spell-checker owl told me there is an abstract noun leak in Biblios. Is this true?'

The leader's bushy eyebrows drew closer. The Uncountables near their leader frowned. The frown spread to the faces of all the Uncountables.

The leader said, 'What you heard is true. We must hurry. The negative abstract nouns are spreading. We will walk with you till the gates of Biblios.'

'Is this an accident?' asked P.

'I believe someone has released these abstract nouns in Biblios. On purpose.'

P and the leader walked ahead of the rest.

The leader said, 'As we speak, there is a storm in the Punctuation Grove. If the storm reaches Biblios, it will be a catastrophe. The winds will spread the negative abstract nouns across the whole town. There would be nothing we could do to stop it.'

To reach Biblios, they had to cross the field and go over a hill. Q shook hands with an Uncountable who was walking with him.

'Do you know who we are?' the Uncountable asked.

'No... Well, yes... I've heard about the Uncountables, but... didn't think they existed,' replied Q.

'We are as real as you are. We are the keepers of uncountable nouns.'

'What are uncountable nouns?'

'Uncountable nouns are nouns that cannot be counted. They may be abstract nouns or concrete nouns. For example: *advice, information, equipment, furniture.*'

'Really? I thought *equipment* was, well, a countable noun. Can't I say: three *equipments*?'

The Uncountable raised his bushy eyebrows and glanced at his black shoes. He clenched his fists.

'No! We add an *s* only when it is a countable noun. This is because only a countable noun can be counted.'

They were climbing up the hill.

'So, countable nouns are *shirts, ponytails, beards.* Things like that,' said Q.

'You are right. We use the indefinite articles with singular countable nouns. *A shirt, a ponytail, an apple.* We do not use an indefinite article in front of an uncountable noun.'

'So, I can't say *an equipment*?'

'No, it is just not done! However, you can say—*a piece of equipment.*'

'And how about *advice*? Can I say *a piece of* advice?'

'Yes, you can. You can also use that phrase with other uncountable nouns—*a piece of* furniture, *a piece of* information.'

'Do I have to use the phrase "*a piece of*" whenever I use an uncountable noun?' asked Q.

'There are lots of other expressions we use with uncountable nouns. *Time*. Is it an uncountable noun?'

'Well, I guess it is.'

'I have *some time*,' the Uncountable said.

'I have *little time*.'

'I don't have *much time*.'

'I have *lots of time*.'

'I have *a lot of time*.'

'I have a question about the expressions: "*lots of*" and "*a lot of*". Do they mean the same thing?' said Q.

'Yes, they do.'

They reached the top of the hill. Below them was Biblios—the largest town in the Dimension. Q saw brown slanting roofs, grey smoke curling out of chimneys, and cobblestone streets making criss-cross patterns. In the centre of the town, there was a building that was on a hill. This building towered over all the other buildings in the town. It looked like a castle, and there were trees on its roof. Two birds were flying towards those trees.

Q had spent his whole life in Alphabet Village where there were only twenty-six houses. Now, he was near thousands of houses and people. His knees began to shake a little.

'We must reach before they close the gates,' said the Uncountable.

'Tell me more about uncountable nouns. I remember you told me that I can't use the indefinite articles *a* and *an* with uncountable nouns,' said Q.

'Yes, that is true. However, you can use the definite article *the* depending on the context. Let's talk about money. *Here is the money I owe you.*'

'Ahh… We are not talking about money in general. We are talking about the money which I owe you.'

'*Money* is not everything in life.'

'Mmm… Since we are talking about money in general, we use the zero article before it.'

'You are right. I should warn you about something. You must know this. Some words can be used as an uncountable noun or as a countable noun. It depends on the context.'

'Just when I was beginning to understand….'

'Let's talk about coffee. *I like coffeē.* This means I like coffee in general. You can go to a cafe in Biblios and say: *two coffees, please.* It means that you would like two cups of coffee, one for you and one for your friend, P. See the difference?'

'I think so.'

P and the Leader of the Uncountables were waiting for them by the tall bronze gates of Biblios. On each gate was a large black semicolon. This punctuation mark was the symbol of the town.

'Unfortunately, we cannot go any farther,' said the leader to Q.

'We are the keepers of uncountable nouns. If we fall ill, uncountable nouns will begin to disappear.'

All the Uncountables exchanged worried glances with one and another.

P whispered to Q, 'If they fall ill, then after a few months, uncountable nouns will become scarce. Some may even disappear. Imagine life without *ink*, or *sugar*, or *peace*.'

P cleared his throat.

He said in a loud, clear voice, 'Dear friends, have no fear. Q is with us!'

Thousands and thousands and thousands of bearded faces lit up with hope.

'But, what can I do?' asked Q.

'We don't have much time. We must enter the town before it is dark,' P said.

They were walking down the main street of Biblios. On both sides of the street, there were shops full of items for sale. Q looked at a row of purple boxes that were overflowing with bananas, pineapples, pencils, erasers, notebooks, and commas.

'Those commas! They look so ripe,' said Q.

'Uuuhh,' mumbled P.

He was examining the faces of the people passing by. He was searching for signs of the negative abstract noun leak. When there are negative abstract nouns in the air, people are generally in a bad mood. They become unfriendly.

'Can I buy a comma? I haven't eaten one for a long time and my friends say that in Biblios...,' said Q.

Before them was a scene of madness. There was a group of about thirty men shouting and shoving each other. Everybody seemed to be fighting with everybody else. Down the street, six women stood in a circle, tearing pages from a dictionary and crumpling them. They flung these crumpled balls of paper up into the air. A group of children were stomping on their crayons. Someone tossed a pineapple at a stationery shop's window. The pineapple shattered the window and hit a bookshelf.

P did not expect it to be this bad. He took out a map which the Leader of the Uncountables had given him. Kneeling on one leg, he unfolded the map on the side of the street. Q ducked to avoid an incoming eraser.

'Not many people have seen this map. It's a closely guarded piece of information. See these blue and red lines. These lines represent the pipes that transport abstract nouns throughout the town. The red lines represent the pipes carrying negative abstract nouns,' said P.

'Why do we even need negative abstract nouns?'

A flowerpot landed near them. The soil from the broken pot scattered onto the edge of the map.

'These pipes transport abstract nouns across the Dimension. We use them for heating and cooking. Without them, we would not be able to survive the winter or cook our food. To make heat, we need to have a mixture of positive and negative abstract nouns. We just can't survive without negative abstract nouns,' said P.

His index finger was tracing a blue line. This line represented a pipe carrying positive abstract nouns.

'There certainly has been a leak. Negative abstract nouns are in the air. I suspect someone opened a red pipe. It must have been opened for at least three minutes. You cannot see negative abstract nouns. You cannot smell them. You cannot touch them. But they are in the air. If these nouns spread to other streets, this town will never be the same again. If people are exposed to negative abstract nouns for more than two days, they will have negative thoughts for the rest of their lives.'

'What can I do?'

'You'll have to go farther down the street and open this valve,' said P, pointing to a blue dot on the map.

'But I'll have to go through that mad crowd. Isn't there any other way?'

'On this street, it is the only valve for the pipe carrying positive abstract nouns. There is no other way. All you have to do is open the blue valve for some time.'

'And how much time is some time?'

'Say the alphabet backwards. Close the valve.'

Q thought about how long that would take. *Would it be three minutes or five minutes? Saying the alphabet backwards will take some time.*

'After you close it, come back here as soon as possible. The positive abstract nouns will overpower the negative ones. These people will stop fighting. Biblios will be peaceful again,' said P.

'I understand. Do I go now?'

'There is something more I need to tell you. The blue valve is hidden. Do you see the picture frame over there?'

Yes,' said Q, craning his neck.

'You'll have to take the frame down. You'll see the blue valve. Open the valve for…'

'As long as it takes to say the alphabet backwards. Shall I go?'

'Wait!'

P was watching a flag in a balcony. It was a yellow flag with a black semicolon. The flag was no longer fluttering in the breeze.

'Now is a good time to go. Try not to attract much attention. These people can do anything. The best way to not get influenced by negative abstract nouns is to think happy thoughts. Go!'

Q thought about his friends in Alphabet Village. And he thought about his journey so far. He thrust his hands into his coat pockets, and he strolled down the street. He tried to whistle, but he could not. A teenager sniggered at him. She threw apples at him. One of the apples hit him hard on his belly button. Q changed his pace and ran. He reached the golden picture frame. Instead of a painting in the frame, there was a sentence: *Grammar is in the details.*

Q did not have the time to appreciate this five-word sentence. After lifting the frame, he placed it on the cobblestone street. He saw the blue valve, and he turned it clockwise. An opening from the pipe expanded. He could neither hear nor smell the positive abstract nouns. He hoped these nouns were escaping into the air. He started to say the alphabet backwards: z, y, x....

Somebody on the third floor of a building saw Q. She stroked her chin, wondering what he was mumbling. She went to her bookcase, and she selected the heaviest book that was there. Returning to the window, she hurled it outside. The thesaurus landed at Q's feet. Thud. Q, looking up, gave her a wide smile.

'I know, I know. I do need to spend more time with new and old words. I've been a bit lazy. Thank you!'

Q forgot which letter he was at. He started again: z,y,x... r,q,p... c,b,a. It was time to close the valve. He turned the blue valve counterclockwise.

All the people on the street glared at him. They were certain he was up to some mischief, and they could tell that he was not from Biblios. Three stocky men rolled up their shirt sleeves. They stomped towards him. The rest of the crowd followed them.

While turning the blue valve, Q did not notice the sudden silence behind him.

P pinched the left tip of his moustache. Unfortunately, he could not help Q. Many years ago, P had dealt with a major negative abstract noun leak in the First Conditional Zone. While controlling that leak, he had inhaled some negative abstract nouns. He had been miserable for three days. If he inhaled the negative abstract nouns in Biblios, his mind would have negative thoughts for months.

Q finished closing the blue valve. He whistled the tune from the word-peckers' song:

Give us a word to peck at,

Wrr... Wrr... Wrr...

When he turned around, he saw many furious faces staring at him. He continued to whistle. A gust of wind blew through the street, throwing up a swirl of leaves.

A man grabbed Q's collar. He shook it hard. After a few seconds, the man's eyes softened. The positive abstract nouns were spreading in the air. Letting go of the collar, he gave Q a toothy grin. The crowd cheered and surrounded him. There were many outstretched hands for Q to shake. Five people hugged him. The lady who threw the thesaurus emerged from the crowd. She presented him with a bowl of commas and cream. Warm tears of joy rolled down her cheeks. Two men raised him onto their shoulders. Children shouted: 'Hurray! Hurray!' There was a celebratory procession to the most important building in town—the Grand Library.

For the people of Biblios, Q was their hero.

Chapter 6

The Pools of the Present

Q was sound asleep in a room lined with freshly printed books. Bright morning sunlight streamed in through a window. On the third shelf, beside the window, there was a book. During the night, this book shook from time to time. A sharp knock on the door woke Q up.

'Sorry to disturb you. My name is K. I am the Grand Librarian.'

'Nice to meet you. I'm Q.'

'May I come in? I am searching for a book.'

'Please.'

K's intelligent eyes surveyed the bookshelves in the room. He focused on the books near the window. He eyed a red hardcover book titled—*The Future Time with Ha*. He snatched the book and placed it on the reading table.

K whispered, 'Ha! I've found you, my word-munching friend.'

He turned the pages slowly. Finally, on page ninety-nine, he found what he was searching for.

'I present to you a grammatical creature.'

Q looked at page ninety-nine. He started from the first sentence and skimmed the page. There, in the middle of the fourth paragraph, was a bookworm. It was as long as this sentence. (Yes, the one before this one.)

'Ehmm… Excuse me, Wow,' said K. 'We have a guest.'

The bookworm finished the sentence it was reading, and it adjusted its golden spectacles. It walked to the beginning of the paragraph. It turned around.

Q said, 'Q.'

'Wow,' said the bookworm.

'Your name is an interjection!'

'It is true.'

'The tree representing interjections told me about a bookworm named Wow.'

'I see you have been to the Circle of Magic Trees. I haven't been there for a long time. I miss the grumpy tree.'

'How did you get your name?'

'I was born on a bookmark in a second-hand bookshop in Writers' Block. Just after I was born, I crawled to the edge of the bookmark. I saw an open book of fairy tales. I read aloud the title of a story. Everyone was stunned. You see, no one taught me how to read the alphabet. It came naturally to me. Anyways, after I read my first sentence, they all exclaimed at the same time: wow! At that moment, my parents decided that was to be my name.'

K said, 'Our guest has not had breakfast. Let us leave.'

'Breakfast is very important,' said Wow.

K placed a purple book next to the book the bookworm was on.

'Your breakfast,' said K.

Keeping its head in the same place, the bookworm raised its body and brought it forward. It was in the shape of an upside-down U. It then lifted its head and stretched out. In this way, the bookworm made its way across page ninety-nine and onto the purple book.

'I always stretch in the morning,' explained Wow.

'Our bookworm is a bit lazy. This is its exercise for the whole day.'

'It isn't easy,' said Wow. 'Why don't you try it?'

'Hurry up. There are lots of adverbs in this book.'

'Yum, yum!' exclaimed Wow, moving faster.

K said to Q, 'Breakfast is in the main reading hall, at the end of the Cookbook Section.'

After having a hot shower, Q put on a fresh pair of clothes. He wandered through the passageways of the Grand Library until he found an enormous oval-shaped hall whose walls were covered with rows and rows of books. After every two bookcases, there was a tall blue window. The blue light from these windows lit up the entire hall. The windows reached up to the high ceiling that was covered with a painting representing eleven grammarians. The grammarians were doing all sorts of things. A grammarian, who had long flowing grey hair, held a paintbrush. She was painting a grammatica flower, whose petals were in different colours. Four grammarians were playing a game of football. A grammarian with a thick black beard was cooking something in a pot. He took a sip from a wooden spoon.

The rows of bookcases were divided into nine levels. On each level, there was a wide platform where library members could stand, sit, and browse. Narrow staircases connected all the levels. Word-peckers were gliding from one level to another.

Q found the Cookbook Section. Passing a sub-section titled *Easy Recipes for Husbands*, he saw a wide balcony where P and K were having breakfast.

'P, as you know, we cannot open the Pools of the Present to our library members. It would be far too risky. Ahh... Q, please have a seat. May I offer you some freshly brewed black coffee?' said K.

'What are the Pools of the Present?' asked Q.

P replied, 'They contain the present tense inside them. There are two underground springs below the Grand Library which supply this special ink. That's why the Grand Library was built on this very spot.'

'Q, could you imagine what would happen if we did not take care of these pools? If the Pools of the Present are disturbed in any way, it may not be possible to use the present tense,' said K.

'We use the present tense all the time in everyday speech,' said P, as he applied some butter on his toast.

'Without the present tense, you could not ask for anything. For instance, you could not ask me to pass you that plate of butter. Now, what kind of world would that be?' said K.

'Don't worry. Our friend K enjoys shocking people. He would never do anything to prevent us from using the present tense,' said P.

'Most certainly not... Never. I would sacrifice my life to protect the pools,' said K.

Q talked about the places he had visited: the Articles Station and the Circle of Magic Trees. K wanted to know why Q had written an article questioning the importance of grammar.

After they finished breakfast, K called out to a word-pecker. The bird was carrying an old book whose cover was tattered. K lovingly inspected the book; he asked the bird to leave it with him. He was going to rebind the book when he had some free time.

'K is one of the most respected grammarians in the Dimension. Even the Grammar Wizard asks him for advice on grammar. He is on the Grammar Council,' whispered P to Q.

From the balcony, Q had a good view of the main gate. Some library members were entering the Grand Library. Soon, the trickle of members became a flood. This flood included babies, children, teenagers, and men and women of all ages.

K said, 'You seem a bit surprised to see so many of our members, so early in the day.'

'Why are all these people here?' asked Q.

'The library is the very heart of our town. We have a nursery, a grammar school, and a gymnasium. Last week, we even had a wedding ceremony right here, in the Cookbook section. In Biblios, everyone wants to spend time at the library. Follow me. I shall show you one of my favourite places,' said K.

They climbed a wrought-iron staircase that zigzagged all the nine levels of the hall. Q saw rows and rows of bookshelves on each level. P envied the word-peckers gliding above him. Every few minutes he would stop and use his handkerchief to wipe off the sweat from his forehead.

They reached the garden. It covered the entire roof of the Grand Library. On the far side, there were six orange trees. Closer to Q, there was a marble fountain that was in the shape of two ink pots. One ink pot was on a raised, tilted platform. Green ink from that pot flowed into the pot which was below. The hedges, which criss-crossed the garden, created lots of corners where one could read without being disturbed.

K said, 'See those library members over there.'

Three women were taking out paintbrushes and bottles of ink from a bag.

'They are going to paint on book covers. You may not have had time to browse through our collection of books. Most of our books have blank covers. When a library member enjoys reading a book, she comes here to paint its cover,' explained K.

K, P, and Q strolled towards the orange trees. Two spell-checker owls were perched at the edge of the murmuring fountain, gazing at their reflections in the ripples of green ink.

P said, 'Those owls are from the Word Fields. They've come here to get ideas for making new sentences,'

K sat down on the grass to speak to a group of children. They begged him to read a story to them. He placed a child on his lap. While K was reading to them, the child tugged at K's grizzled beard.

Taking in the fragrance of oranges, Q stood near a tree and gazed at the buildings below. P surveyed the garden with a satisfied smile. Not many people knew this, but it was his idea to have a rooftop garden for the library.

'Guess what? All the word-peckers lived happily ever after in the Punctuation Grove,' said K.

The children clapped their hands.

'Another story, please, please, please,' said the child on K's lap.

K glanced at P.

'I want a one-minute story,' said another child.

'One-minute story, one-minute story, one-minute story', the children chanted.

P said, 'K, I think we should show Q the pools.'

'Tomorrow, I promise. Tomorrow,' said K to the children.

K, P, and Q came down the staircase, passing many library members on the different levels. K politely greeted everyone. He asked a few members what books they were searching for. When he reached the Reference Section, he selected a purple book. With the book in his hand, they reached the ground floor. K asked P and Q to follow him into a small room. There was a passageway. It spiralled downwards, deep under the main reading hall.

'To your left, we have the personal reading rooms. To your right, the dreaming rooms,' said K.

'Dreaming rooms?' asked Q.

K pulled back a heavy curtain to reveal a dreaming room. In this room, everything was orange: the walls, the bedstand, the mattress, the pillows, and the round table.

'You place the book you want to "read" on the table and fall asleep. You dream your book,' explained K. 'The dream usually lasts for a few hours, depending on the length of the book and the power of your imagination. When people wake up, they make a few notes. As you know, after some time, we forget our dreams.'

'Do lots of people use dreaming rooms?' asked Q.

'People get to know books and stories in different ways. Some like to read them. Some like to listen to them. Some like to dream them.'

The passageway was getting narrower: they had to walk in single file. They climbed down a set of steep steps and reached a thick wooden door. K took out a bunch of keys. He unlocked the door and pushed hard to open it.

He announced, 'Welcome to the Pools of the Present!'

They entered an underground cave. The echo of moving ink splashing on stone filled their ears. The ground was covered with pebbles and sharp rocks. They had to walk carefully. Although there were lanterns on the uneven walls, at some places it was quite dark. When they came to the first pool, K opened the book he was carrying.

'Wow, would you like to introduce the pools to our guest?'

The bookworm looked a little fatter than when Q saw it before.

'My, those adverbs were tasty. Oh… Hello again Q. P! How are you? Good to see you. Yes, so we are at the Pools of the Present. Without them we would not be able to use the present tense and the present continuous. The ink here is unique,' said Wow.

'What happens if this ink disappears? How would we talk without using the present tense?' asked Q.

'Well, you could use hand gestures. You could also draw what you want to express. But, yes, communicating with others will not be easy.'

'I hope these pools will be here forever.'

'Now, the pool in front of us holds the present simple tense. We use the present simple to talk about something that is generally true.'

'*I live in Alphabet Village,*' said Q.

'Yes, that's in the present simple. We also use the present simple to talk about scientific facts.'

'*The sun rises in the east.*'

'Yes. We also use the present simple to talk about something that happens many times in the present period,' said Wow. '*I eat adverbs.*'

'I *sometimes* eat adverbs. Is it also in the present simple?'

'It is. Apart from using the adverb *sometimes*, we can use other adverbs such as *often* and *always*.'

'Okay.'

'Don't forget, if you use the third person singular, such as *he*, *she*, or *it*, we normally add an *s* at the end of the verb. *She swims in the river,*' said Wow.

'But not all verbs follow this rule. Sometimes we add an '*es*' to the verb. S*he teaches creative writing*,' said Q.

'That's right. There are irregular verbs as well. What are the forms for the verb: *to be?*'

'*I am, you are, she is, he is, it is, we are, you are, they are.*'

'Exactly.'

'Can I touch the ink?'

'Go ahead.'

Q dipped his hands into the pool. His body shivered and skin tingled. The ink was ice cold, but there was something else as well.

'I can't describe the feeling.'

'This ink is indescribable. It has the present simple tense inside it, after all. Now, if you want to make questions in the present simple, you use the auxiliaries *do* and *does*. Make some questions for us,' said Wow.

Q asked, '*Do bookworms read? Does our bookworm read?*'

'I read a book a day. We don't just eat words.'

P and K stepped away to have a private conversation. Their long shadows moved on the wall.

'We use "*do not*" and "*does not*" to make negative sentences,' said Wow.

'*I do not read. He does not read.*'

'That's right. Remember, when we speak with friends, we normally use contractions. *She doesn't read. He doesn't read.*'

Q was making notes. The blue glow of the pool gave him enough light to write.

P asked, 'Do you have a good idea of how to use the present simple?'

'I do,' replied Q.

'Time to visit the next pool. If it's alright with you, Wow,' P said.

'Why wouldn't it be? Could you take me there?'

Q held the open book in both hands. The bookworm rested on its back. Stretching itself across a simple sentence, it yawned.

'Wait!' screamed Q.

Wait... wait... wait... His voice echoed from the stone walls. He had seen a flash of yellow and orange in the blue ink.

'What is it?' asked Wow.

'I saw something moving in the ink,' said Q.

Wow rolled over and decided not to stand up.

'Goldfish live here.'

Q went closer to the pool. He could make out the form of a goldfish darting in the glowing blue ink. He saw another one, and then another one.

'So, there may be a connection between the present simple tense and goldfish,' said Q.

'It's what some people say,' said Wow. 'I'm not sure, though.'

'I feed the fish every day. I take good care of them,' said K.

In the next pool, the ink was green and sparkling. It was moving fast, forming a whirlpool. Q saw goldfish in it; some goldfish were swimming against the current.

Wow said, 'I just love the energy of the present continuous tense. Nothing quite like it! We use this tense to talk about things we are doing right now, for a temporary period of time. For example: I *am eating* some delicious adverbs.'

'You are supposed to be on a diet, 'said K, 'Remember, you promised.'

'We also use the present continuous to talk about an action that is not happening right now, but it is happening around the present moment. *I am reading a book on goldfish.* I may not be reading the book at this very moment, but I am reading it these days. Again, it is a temporary action,' Wow said.

'Any other uses of the present continuous? Our guests have to leave soon,' said K.

'We also use the present continuous to talk about something that is changing or growing,' said Wow.

'My knowledge of grammar *is improving*,' said Q.

'That could be true,' said Wow. 'The form of the present continuous is—*am/are/is + ing form of the verb.*'

'And *am/are/is* are all forms of the verb *be.*'

'There is one more use of this tense I want to talk about. That is when we use the present continuous to talk about things that will happen in the future. But, the best place for you to learn about it is when you are in the Garden of Grammar. Please, reach there in time, before it is too late.'

'Before it is too late for what?' asked K.

'I can read between the lines. There are whispers of anti-grammatical forces in the Dimension. That's the reason why all of you are here, at the pools. P and Q are on their way to meet the Grammar Wizard,' said Wow.

'Anti-grammatical forces?' said K.

Wow said to Q, 'Never ever judge a book by its cover.'

The bookworm dived deep into the white space of the page's left margin. Q gently closed the book.

K said, 'I shall take that from you. Thank you.'

While they were climbing the stairs, Q saw that all the dreaming rooms were occupied. A man, who had woken up from his dream, was shouting: 'What an amazing idea! Why didn't I think of it?'

They reached the main reading hall.

'Please excuse me. I need to meet some library members. Do have a look around,' said K.

P and Q browsed the books on the first level.

A word-pecker landed on the railing.

'May... wrr... I help you?'

'I'm searching for a good book on the present simple tense,' Q replied.

The bird flew to the sixth level. It returned with a slim book in its light-blue beak. On the spine of the book was the title: *Goldfish in the Pools of the Present.*

'Just what I was looking for,' said Q.

The word-pecker flew away, cooing, 'Wrr... Wrr...'

Q was surprised to read P's name on the third page. According to the book, P was the first person who said that the goldfish must be fed every day.

K returned to the main reading hall which was teeming with people. He could not see his guests. He asked a word-pecker to find them. Q was still on the first level, while P was on the third level. The word-pecker told them that K was searching for them.

'A spell-checker owl has given me a message from the Grammar Wizard. She wants to meet both of you at her cottage, tomorrow evening after sunset,' said K.

'It seems Wow was right after all. We will be in the Garden of Grammar,' said P.

'You must have been there many times.'

'Actually, I've never been there. Not even once.'

Usually, the Grammar Wizard asked spell-checker owls to pass on her instructions to P.

'Mmm... Even after being in her service for all these many years?' asked K.

'She has never called me to her cottage.'

'Our Grammar Wizard is mysterious, isn't she?'

'Before we leave, it would be a good idea to visit the Memory Store.'

'I absolutely agree. Before going to the Garden of Grammar, Q needs to know a little about our past.'

CHAPTER 7

The Memory Store:
The Past Tense

On the street, two girls shouted: 'Thank you!' Q mumbled something to them. A young man shyly asked him for his autograph. Q blushed.

'You're a star now. Act like one,' said P.

'I don't feel like one,' said Q, before signing his name on a piece of paper.

You may surprise yourself one day, P thought.

Taking a left turn from the main street, they entered a quiet neighbourhood. Q felt that the air was different here: it was heavier.

'Where are we?'

'Writers' Block. This is where writers stay when they find it difficult to write.'

A policeman, the only other person on the street, approached them. He looked deep into their eyes.

'Only those with a valid poetic licence are allowed in Writers' Block. Gentlemen, may I see yours?'

P showed his licence. According to the licence, he was qualified to write all forms of poetry.

The policeman smiled when he recognised Q.

'It is a privilege to meet the person who has saved our town.'

Giving them a smart salute, the policeman said, 'If you need any help, let me know.'

They strolled down the street. The click-click-click sound of a typewriter came from a half-opened door. In a cafe, two writers were having a lively conversation on when to use a comma.

P turned into a lane. He looked fondly at a dusty shop window. Thick glass jars were on display. In some jars, there was a green liquid. In other jars, the liquid was blue.

'This is where you store your memories. There's a friend of mine I want you to meet,' said P.

As he pushed the door, a bell rang.

'My dear P, how are you?' a deep voice boomed.

Q peered into the shop, searching for the owner of the voice. All he saw were rows and rows of jars.

P said, 'Woz! It has been a while.'

'I thought of you when I was carrying your memory jar the other day. Yes, it was the other day. Would you like to see it?'

'This visit is for my friend Q. He wants to know how you store memories.'

'Pleasure to meet you, Q. Woz is the name.'

Q finally found P's friend. He was no taller than the pile of four jars next to him. He gave Q a firm handshake. They walked into a damp room.

Using a step ladder, Woz climbed onto a stool. His bald head reflected the candlelight around them.

'Memory is what holds the Grammar Dimension together. Yes. It is a correct statement,' said Woz. 'The Memory Store has been here for as long as anyone can remember. My mother used to run this place before me. Before that, it was her father. Before that it was… Umm… P, you really should open your memory jar. It has come out very well. It's over there.'

Making a thumbs-up sign, P went in search of his jar.

'And how is a memory jar made?' asked Q.

'A customer gives us an object that is related to a specific memory. Umm… The object could be a postcard, or a bookmark, or a piece of cloth. Anything which is related to the memory. I place the object into a jar of ink.'

Woz scratched the top of his pointy ear.

'Umm… Where was I? Yes, the process. First, I pour some ink in the jar. Then I place the object in it. Once the object is in the jar, I add three drops of ink from the Pools of the Present. Not a drop extra. After twenty-one days, the object in the jar melts. It turns into a liquid. I add some soil from the Garden of Grammar. One teaspoon will do. The jar starts to turn yellow. This is a sign that the memory is being formed. Once the jar is so yellow that I cannot see what is inside, I know this memory will be stored for all time.'

Q glanced at the memory jars around him. They were in different shades of yellow.

'But how do people re-live their memories from these jars?'

'Umm… You open the lid of the jar, breathe deeply, take in the aromas.'

'Really?'

'Breathe deeply through your nose. This is the important part. Once the aromas hit you, you will remember everything as it once was. My job is done! There is one thing you have to know, though, for all of this to work.'

'What is it?'

'Why, you need to know the past simple tense and the past continuous tense, umm… naturally,' replied Woz, grinning from pointy ear to pointy ear.

'Could you tell Q how to talk about the past?' asked P, from the other side of the store.

Woz said, 'Certainly… We use the past simple to talk about an action that happened over a period of time in the past. *I lived in Biblios.*'

'Okay,' said Q.

'We also use the past simple to talk about something that happened for a short duration of time in the past,' said Woz.

'I *talked* with a bookworm.'

'Verbs such as *lived, walked,* and *talked* are called regular verbs. We make the past tense form by adding *-d* or *-ed* to their base form.'

'And there are irregular verbs as well, for example, *go* becomes *went,* and *write* becomes *wrote,*' said Q.

'The verb "*to be*" is irregular. Could you tell me the past forms of this verb?'

'*Was* and *were*… Yesterday, I *was* at the Circle of Magic Trees. Yesterday, we *were* at the Circle of Magic Trees.'

'The magic trees. I met all those magnificent trees many years ago. It was in the Year of the Question Mark. Or was it the Year of the Apostrophe? Back to the present. Umm… I mean the past simple. If you want to make a negative statement in the past simple, use "*did not*". If you are speaking informally, use "*didn't*".'

'He *did not visit* the Circle of Magic Trees. He *didn't visit* the Circle of Magic Trees.'

'Could you make a question in the past simple?'

'*Did* he *visit* the Circle of Magic Trees?'

'Yes, yes… *did I, did you, did we, did they*. Enough about the past simple. Time to talk about the past continuous tense,' said Woz.

'I don't know anything about the past continuous.'

P was reading the labels on a row of memory jars. The label of a memory jar gave the following information: name of the owner of the memory, where the memory was made, and the base emotion of the memory (for example: happiness).

There was a jar on which the owner's name was blackened out. P held this jar next to a burning candle. The jar was as yellow as a lemon: it held an old memory. Woz saw P's reflection in a mirror.

'May I help you, old friend?' asked Woz.

'Just looking. Could you tell me whose memory this is?'

'Umm… The customer doesn't want anyone to know whose it is,' replied Woz.

'I understand. Carry on,' said P.

'Alright… Umm… There are many ways to use the past continuous. We'll look at one way. We use the past continuous to talk about an action that happened before and after another action,' said Woz.

'I'm a little lost.'

'*When you were walking over here, a policeman stopped you.*'

'How do you know?'

'The policeman in Writers' Block stops anyone who is not a writer.'

'So, the verb *walking* happened over a period of time in the past. And, during this period, an action happened: a policeman stopped me.'

'This is how we use the past continuous.'

Q wrote the form of the past continuous: *was/were + ing form of the verb*.

Woz said, 'You have written the form correctly. Now, an example?'

'*While I was searching for a word in a dictionary, a spell-checker owl hooted.*'

'Yes, yes... Enough about grammar... I'll talk about some history now. In the beginning, our Dimension was in chaos. Chaos... Yes, that's a good word to describe how it was. There were negative abstract nouns floating everywhere. Oh, the horror! Umm... There were no grammar rules. None at all... Can you believe it? When people wrote letters to each other, their messages were often misunderstood. There were fights all the time. Out of all this confusion, the first Grammar Wizard appeared. He brought order to the Dimension. Unfortunately, a few people became jealous of him and plotted against him. They did not succeed. This happened a long time ago, but the past repeats itself. Umm... In different ways, of course, but the past does repeat itself. This is what I wanted to say to you.'

P came up from behind and grasped Woz's thin shoulders.

'Time for us to leave,' said P.

'Have dinner with me and the family.'

'Some other time. I promise.'

Pointing at some empty jars, Woz said, 'Remember this Q. When all else fails, memory can save you.'

They were walking through the streets of Writers' Block. They waved at the policeman who had stopped them before.

'While you were talking with Woz, I opened someone's memory jar,' P whispered.

'Are you allowed to do that?' asked Q.

'Well, one is not supposed to do it, at least not without the owner's permission. It's not a polite thing to do. The label on the jar drew me to it. When I opened the lid, I took in some strong aromas.'

'What were they?'

'Wet earth, wood, and apples.'

'And you could smell all these aromas separately?'

'Yes. I only wish I knew what those aromas added up to.'

'Did Woz know what you were doing?'

'Oh, he did. The memory jar was above mine. Woz wanted to warn me.'

Chapter 8

Ha to the Future

The Dimension Mountain Range, the source of all visible ink, was in the distance. It consisted of four mountains, and it marked the northern boundary of the Garden of Grammar. Black and red clouds were in the sky. Below the balloon, there were blue, black, red, and green flowers as far as the eye could see. Trees of all shapes and sizes dotted the landscape.

'All the flowers look the same,' said Q.

'They are grammatica flowers,' said P.

'The grammatica flower. The official symbol of the Grammar Wizard.'

'Whenever I get an envelope from the Grammar Wizard, it is always sealed with the image of this flower.'

They landed softly in the garden. P was not sure which path to take to reach the cottage. He chose one that went along the River of Blue Ink.

Q sniffed the flowers.

'The blue flowers smell differently from the green ones.'

'You are becoming sensitive to grammar.'

'Ha! If only....'

A tall man appeared from behind a tree. Crossing his arms, he planted his legs firmly on the ground.

'You called my name?'

Q felt a lump in his throat when he saw the man's muscles.

'I... I did not call your... your name,' said Q.

'My name is Ha. You called my name.'

'It is a pleasure to meet you. I've heard so much about you. My name is P.'

'P, I have heard so much about you. Welcome to the Garden of Grammar!'

'Ha is the guardian of the Garden of Grammar. He is one of the strongest men in the entire Dimension, and he is also a famous grammarian. Ha has written nine books on grammar,' said P.

'I think I saw one of your books at the Grand Library. It was about the future time,' said Q.

'I have written two books on the future time.'

P said, 'Ha, I've never been here before. Could you show us the way to the cottage?'

'Please wait here. I will tell the Grammar Wizard you have arrived.'

P and Q admired a bed of green grammatica flowers. Q observed the moving petals of a flower. The petals curled in and they straightened out. It happened very slowly. The petals did not move together: each petal moved at its own speed.

'The grammatica flower has eight petals. Each petal represents a part of speech,' said P.

Q placed his hand above a flower. Its moving petals brushed his palm, tickling him gently.

Ha returned and said, 'The Grammar Wizard is delighted to know that you are here. She is expecting to see you after sunset.'

P said, 'We have some time. Q has been exploring different parts of the Dimension, and he has been having conversations about grammar. Could you tell him about the future time?'

'Certainly… Follow me, Q,' Ha said. 'We will sit by a stream of red ink.'

'I already know how to talk about the future, but I'd be happy to listen to you,' said Q.

When they reached the stream, Ha said, 'Have some ink. It will refresh you.'

Scooping up some ink, Q drank it quickly.

'It's so fresh!'

'It is melted snow from the mountains. Could you tell me how one can talk about the future?'

Q dried his hands by rubbing them together. There was a light red stain on his fingernails.

'I use *will*. I *will* drink some more red ink.'

'Yes, at the moment of speaking, one uses *will* to talk about something one decides to do in the future. If one is talking informally, one usually uses the contraction of *will*. *I'll* drink some more red ink.'

Q asked, 'Are there any other uses of *will*?'

'We also use *will* when we make a promise.'

'Hmm... Sometimes I tell my wife this: I *will* make dinner tonight.'

'That can be taken as a promise,' said Ha.

'I *won't* make dinner tonight. This is about the future as well. Right?'

'Yes, it is. The negative form of *will* is *won't*. *Won't* is a contraction of *will not*.'

'What is the form of *will*?'

'The form is: *will + infinitive without to*,' said Ha.

'Hmm... Can you give me some examples of infinitives?'

'To read. To go. To sleep.'

'Ahh... Interesting. All these verbs have a 'to' in front of them. You said the form of will is *will + infinitive without to*. So, that would be—*will read... won't go... will sleep*.'

'Yes. When we write formally, we do not use *won't*. We use *will not*.'

'So, when I write a letter to the mayor, I shouldn't use *won't*. Right?' said Q.

'That is correct.'

Q stood up and dusted his pants.

'Well, thank you. I enjoyed the lesson.'

Stroking his light beard thoughtfully, Ha raised a bushy eyebrow.

'Where are you going?'

'Haven't we finished talking about the future?'

Ha laughed from his belly. Ha ha ha!

'We have just begun. There are so many other ways to talk about the future.'

'I thought that was it. We spoke about *will*. What else can there be?'

'There is so much more. We use *shall* when we decide to do something or make a promise. Actually, we use *shall* in the same way we use *will*.'

'I *shall* be there.'

'I *shall not* be there. That is the negative form of *shall*,' said Ha.

'And with friends we usually use the contraction. I *shan't* be there,' said Q.

'That is correct. Let's talk about another use. We often use *shall* when we want to make an offer.'

'*Shall* I get some red ink for you?' asked Q.

'We also use *shall* to make a suggestion. *Shall* we talk some more about the future time?'

Sitting down again, Q dipped his hand in the stream of ink.

'*You shall bring me some ink.* That just sounds rude.'

'It sounds as if you are commanding the person to bring you some ink. Usually, when we use the verb *shall*, we use it only with the first-person pronouns, *I* and *we*,' said Ha.

'I shall remember that. What's the form?'

'*Shall + infinitive without to.*'

Q jotted it down.

'There are many other uses of *will* and *shall*. If you want to know more, you could always read my books,' said Ha.

Q was silent as he was reading his notes.

'Do you have any questions?' asked Ha.

'Is there a difference between *will* and *shall*?'

'When you feel strongly about something, I suggest you use *will* instead of *shall*.'

'I *will* protect the Pools of the Present,' said Q.

'That is a good use of *will*. Could you think of any other way to talk about the future?'

'No, not really...'

'Look up. Tell me what you see.'

'I see dark red clouds.'

'What do you think could happen?' asked Ha.

'It is *going to* rain.'

'You have just said something about the future.'

'Ahhh... So, we use *going to* when we want to talk about the future.'

'We use *going to* to talk about something we feel has a good chance of happening because there is some evidence,' explained Ha, 'For instance, since you see the dark clouds, you predict it is going to rain.'

'I see how it works. But, isn't there another way of using *going to*? *We are going to see the Grammar Wizard this evening.*'

'That is another use of the phrase *going to*. When we have made a decision in the past, and we are talking about it now, we use *going to*.'

Q said, 'And the form is: *going to + infinitive without to*.'

'Yes.'

Q ran his fingers through his curly hair.

'What's the difference between these two sentences? We *will* meet the Grammar Wizard this evening. We are *going to* meet the Grammar Wizard this evening.'

'When we use the verb *will*, it means that we decide right now, at the time of speaking, to go and meet the Grammar Wizard in the evening,' said Ha.

'Okay.'

'*We are going to meet the Grammar Wizard this evening.* Here, we are talking about a decision that we have already made.'

'Not clear,' said Q, with a slight frown.

'In the morning, we, you and I, agree to go and meet the Grammar Wizard in the evening. In the afternoon, we meet P. We tell him: We *are going to meet* the Grammar Wizard this evening.'

'Ah! So, when we meet P in the afternoon, we are telling him about something we have already decided to do. Now, it makes sense.'

'Yes.'

Q wrote down the difference between *will* and *going to*.

'Could you think of any other way to talk about the future?' asked Ha.

'Not really...'

'We use the present continuous tense to talk about the future.'

'Mmm... Wow told me I'll learn about this in the Garden of Grammar. When I was at the Grand Library, Wow was sleeping in one of your books.'

'Wow enjoys eating prepositions. In four of my books, there are blank spaces where prepositions used to be. What to do!'

'Wow also likes eating adverbs.'

'Let's talk some more about the present continuous. We use it to talk about plans or arrangements in the future that are already fixed or arranged. *We are meeting the Grammar Wizard this evening.*'

'We are *going to* meet the Grammar Wizard this evening. Can't I just say that?'

'Yes, you can,' said Ha. 'But, there is a difference in meaning. *We are going to meet the Grammar Wizard this evening.* This means that we have decided to meet her'.

'Okay.'

'We *are meeting* the Grammar Wizard this evening. This means that we have an appointment with her: she is expecting us.'

'Ah... I see the difference. I remember what the form of the present continuous is—*am/is/are + ing form of the verb*.'

'Correct. It is interesting to note that we also use the present simple tense to talk about the future,' said Ha.

'How can I use the *present* simple to talk about the *future*?'

'We use the present simple for something that we are sure will happen in the future.'

'For example?' asked Q.

'We *leave* tomorrow morning.'

'Ahhh... It means we have made all the preparations for leaving tomorrow.'

'Yes. We also use the present simple when there is a fixed schedule,' said Ha.

'How?'

'The library *opens* at nine o'clock on Sunday.'

'It opens every Sunday at nine o'clock. And we are sure it will open at nine o'clock this Sunday as well.'

'Yes.'

Q went over his notes.

'So, to talk about the future time, we use—*will, shall, going to,* the *present continuous,* and the *present simple.*'

'Yes.'

'Is there anything else I need to know about the future time?'

A spell-checker owl's feather twirled down from the sky. The brown feather landed on the stream of red ink. The flowing ink carried the feather away from them.

Ha said, 'I should tell you about the future continuous tense as well.'

'What is that?'

'We use the future continuous to talk about something that will be going on at a particular moment, or over a period of time, in the future.'

'And I thought I knew everything about the future time.'

'This evening, you *will be meeting* the Grammar Wizard.'

'Mmm… So, something will be happening during a period of time in the future. I will be meeting the Grammar Wizard,' said Q.

'Yes.'

'At seven o'clock in the morning, I *will be having* breakfast.'

'That is correct. At a particular time in the future, at seven o'clock in the morning, you will be having breakfast. I am glad you make your own sentences. Could you make a negative statement using the future continuous?'

'*At seven o'clock in the morning, I won't be having breakfast.* And if I want to be formal: *At seven o'clock in the morning, I will not be having breakfast.*'

'What is the form of the future continuous?' asked Ha.

'*Will be + ing form of the verb.*'

'Well done. You have a good idea of the future time. It is time to meet the Grammar Wizard. Let us find your friend.'

When they saw P, he was trying to have a conversation with a bed of grammatica flowers.

'I feel I can communicate with you. Can you hear me?'

He blushed a bit when Ha and Q suddenly appeared in front of him.

'Ever since I entered the garden, I've been hearing a humming sound. It is so soothing. Never heard it before,' said P.

'You have a good ear for grammar. The flowers hum in the evening,' said Ha.

'How come I can't hear anything?' asked Q.

'You will. Give yourself some time,' said Ha.

'Why do their petals move?' asked P. 'I've seen grammatica flowers before. They never did this.'

The petals were curling in and stretching out.

'These flowers are in the soil of the Garden of Grammar. That's why they behave like this. The petals move when it turns dusk. They stop moving when the stars are out.'

They walked deeper into the garden. Q saw a nest in a tree. The nest was made of interwoven tattered bookmarks. He jumped up, catching a glimpse of three eggs. They were light blue and were covered with brown spots. Inside the nest, a children's poetry book was opened to pages nine and ten.

'Those are spell-checker owl eggs,' said Ha. 'The mother was reading from that book.'

'Do mother owls spell words to their chicks even when they are still in their eggs?' asked Q.

'They do… I, myself, sometimes spell words to the eggs. When I finish spelling a difficult word, the eggs wobble a bit. Spelling words to them helps the chicks to become grammatical creatures,' said Ha.

'And what exactly are grammatical creatures?'

'Grammatical creatures have a strong bond with the Garden of Grammar. They feel the energy of grammar. They love grammar and see it everywhere, in everything. It's a bit difficult to put into words.'

'And is it true that the Circle of Magic Trees and the Garden of Grammar are physically connected? I never believed it.'

'The roots of the trees here touch the roots of the trees there.'

They arrived at the Grammar Wizard's two-storey cottage.

Ha turned right and walked away from them.

'See you soon, my friends.'

P asked, 'How do we let the Grammar Wizard know we are here?'

'Try knocking on the door.'

P's heart was pounding—thump, thump, thump.

CHAPTER 9

The Perfect Dream: Present Perfect

Her kind eyes were framed by a pair of black spectacles. Her gown was silvery grey, like the colour of the moon on a misty evening. She had straight grey hair that reached down to her waist. Around her neck was a string of pink pearls. On her chin, there was a black beauty mark, as round as a full stop.

P and Q were speechless.

'Welcome to our home. Please do come in,' she said.

Q looked around the cottage. An empty rocking chair was rocking, and it was slowly coming to a halt. Near an orange sofa, there was a winding staircase. Beside a bookcase, a sentence, written in silver, was in a wooden picture frame. The sentence was—*Listen to the sound of the river of invisible ink.*

She asked them to sit at the round table. Three empty cups were on it.

'Thank you for coming. My assistant will join us shortly. Let me introduce myself. I am the Grammar Wizard.'

'It is an honour to meet you, Grammar Wizard. I am P. This is Q. The Grand Librarian said you wished to see us. How may we be of service?'

Holding a teapot, the Grammar Wizard poured green tea into the orange cups. She served P and Q. She wrapped her hands around her favourite cup. It was an orange teacup with golden zigzag lines painted across it.

'What can I say? It seems someone wants to destroy our world.'

'I am certain someone purposely released negative abstract nouns in Biblios,' said P.

'Oh, yes… There was the negative abstract noun leak. There have been other incidents as well. Yesterday, two towers at the Articles Station collapsed.'

'We were there just a few days ago,' said P, 'What happened?'

'Late last night, someone placed many incorrect words in the two towers for indefinite articles. When Maz arrived in the morning, she saw a terrible sight. One tower had snapped into two and another tower had collapsed, breaking into pieces.'

P noticed that she raised her left eyebrow whenever she stressed a word. She raised it when she said the words *incorrect*, *snapped*, and *collapsed*.

'Is Maz alright?' asked Q.

'She sent me a letter saying she is fine. Two members from the Grammar Council are already at the Articles Station. Spell-checker owls from the Word Fields are there too. They are helping her to rebuild the towers.'

'Has anything else happened?' asked P.

'Three days ago, a group of relative clauses went missing from the Word Fields. This has never happened before. The spell-checker owls are so upset. The owls asked me for some advice on what to do. I had nothing to tell them.'

P took a sip of green tea from his cup.

'What can we do?'

'At the present moment, the best thing to do is to have dinner.'

Lamp of Grammar

A woman glided down the staircase. She wore a silvery gown, like the Grammar Wizard's. She had long wavy hair. Two marks, one above the other, were on her chin. They looked like a punctuation mark: a colon.

'My dear, let me introduce you to our guests. This is P, who has been serving the Grammar Dimension for many, many years. This young man is Q. Gentlemen, may I present my assistant, M. She is an absolute whiz at grammar, and she is one of the kindest persons I have ever known.'

They greeted each other. Q tried hard not to stare at M. For some reason, he felt that he had met her before. Had he seen her on the rooftop of the Grand Library? Or, was it on the streets of Biblios?

M went to the kitchen and brought some plates, spoons, and glasses. Q helped her set the table.

While dinner was being prepared, the Grammar Wizard stood in front of a lamp. It was between two sets of books in a bookshelf.

She gently wiped the lamp with a white cloth. After lighting the lamp, she placed it at the centre of the table.

P gazed at the lamp without blinking. Its shape and design were that of a spell-checker owl. P felt that the lamp's two owlish eyes were looking straight at him. In all his travels, he had never seen such a lamp before.

They sat down.

'We will talk about the problems facing the Dimension tomorrow. This evening, I want you to eat well and take some rest,' said the Grammar Wizard.

Q fumbled with his spoon. It fell onto the floor.

The Grammar Wizard said, 'You seem a little dazed.'

'I am surprised at how well both of you are dressed. I mean... I thought the Grammar Wizard would not look like... well... You look so glamorous,' said Q.

His cheeks were as red as the tomatoes on his plate. The two women looked at each other sideways and smiled.

'The word *glamour* comes from the word *grammar*. A long time ago, *grammar* meant more than what it means today. It represented all forms of learning, including magic. People thought that a person who knows grammar is mysterious and has many secrets. During this time, some people started to pronounce the word *grammar* differently. They replaced the first *r* in grammar with an *l*. This is how the word *glamour* came from the word *grammar*. So being glamorous is part of our job description, so to say,' said the Grammar Wizard, raising an eyebrow as she said the words *glamour*, *grammar*, and *mysterious*.

'Do you live in the Garden of Grammar?' asked P.

The Grammar Wizard sipped some black ink before answering.

'Well, I do spend some time here. Not that much, though. I travel most of the time. I enjoy listening to how people use grammar in everyday life. I find it fascinating.'

Q said to M, 'Then you must be the one who lives here.'

'Not really. I travel a lot as well. Spell-checker owls pass messages between the Grammar Wizard and me. We stay in touch this way.'

'Q, you would have heard about the Grammar Council. There are seven members on the council. Every month, we meet at the foothills of the Dimension Mountain Range. We always have a lot to discuss. The members share their views on when and where to hold spelling bees. We talk about possible themes for creative writing competitions. We plan out the theatre calendar for the season,' said the Grammar Wizard.

'Do you also make changes to the rules of grammar?' asked Q.

'We do. But it usually takes time. To make a change in the rules of grammar, every member on the council needs to agree. Unfortunately, this does not happen often,' replied the Grammar Wizard.

'I never imagined I'd one day be in the Garden of Grammar,' said Q.

'Many years ago, we extended the garden by planting grammatica seeds. These seeds need silence to grow. So, we did not encourage people to visit us. As the flowers are fully grown, we can now send invitations. In fact, we are celebrating Grammar Day with the children from the Third Conditional Zone,' said the Grammar Wizard.

'I'm sure the children will be thrilled to be here,' said Q.

P said, 'Thank you so much for the dinner. It reminds me of home cooking.'

'Our food is simple and wholesome. I am glad you enjoyed it. It would be a good idea for both of you to take some rest,' said the Grammar Wizard.

M went to the stairs and called out a name. A word-pecker spiralled down from upstairs. It landed on the orange sofa, hitting its head on a cushion.

The bird said, 'Wrr… My name are Woo.'

'Woo will take you to your rooms. We will be here for some more time. If you need anything, please ask Woo. Gentlemen, goodnight and sweet dreams,' said the Grammar Wizard.

P and Q followed the word-pecker up the steps.

'Your rooms is here. Wrr… These two is for you and you.'

P shuddered when he heard Woo's grammatically incorrect sentences. He was shocked to hear such horrible grammar from a word-pecker, and that too in the Garden of Grammar.

Downstairs, the Grammar Wizard and M, the Assistant Grammar Wizard, spoke in hushed voices.

'Did they suspect anything?' asked M, removing her wig.

'I sent them to bed early. I didn't want them to spend more time with us. P is a clever man. He'll notice something, sooner or later,' said the Grammar Wizard.

Holding a hand mirror, she peeled off the dot on her chin.

In his room, P tossed and turned in bed. He was thinking about the way the Grammar Wizard raised her eyebrow. Next door, Q had no problem finding sleep. He was snoring like a spell-checker owl.

'Wake up!'

Q got up with a start. His wife was calling him. He looked around his bedroom. Yes. It was his room: there were his books on the shelf, his clothes in the closet and his red slippers on the floor. *Was the visit to the Garden of Grammar just a dream?*

A sizzling sound came from somewhere. Rubbing his eyes, he stumbled into the kitchen. His wife, N, was at the kitchen counter.

Her back was turned to him. A blue vase, with three grammatica flowers, was on the table. Each flower was of a different colour—black, green, and red. Q had never seen grammatica flowers at home before.

'I had the most amazing dream. There was this person called P who came to our home. And we flew away in the mayor's balloon. I went to the Articles Station. The sky… It was… And then I was at the Circle of Magic Trees. The trees spoke to me! In the breeze… And I was in Biblios. The Grand Library… And I met the Uncountables. They all look the same, by the way. And I met Woz. He told me how to make a memory jar. Then I was with Ha in the Garden of Grammar. Yes, in the Garden of Grammar! I saw spell-checker owl eggs. Two, or maybe three… I really have… I even had dinner with the Grammar Wizard!' said Q, his eyes wide with excitement.

'Have some breakfast, darling,' said N.

Scooping out seeds from a pomegranate, she did not turn to him while speaking.

'How long have I been sleeping for?' asked Q.

'Eat.'

N gave him his favourite breakfast: boiled commas on toast and scrambled eggs. Q forgot about his dream as he gobbled up the food. The plate was so clean that he could see his own reflection. He saw that he had a beard. He touched the prickly hair on his chin. Q wondered how he could have grown such a beard in just one night.

N placed two glasses of pomegranate juice on the table. She picked one up. As she drank from it, her eyes were fixed on her husband.

'What is it?' asked Q.

'You have to be perfect. There is no other way.'

'I don't understand.'

'You have to know about the present perfect tense.'

Bending down, N kissed his forehead. She sat down at the table, and she slid the blue vase with the three flowers to one side.

'We use the present perfect to talk about something that happened in the past, and it has some importance right now,' said N. '*I have had my breakfast*. This means I am not hungry right now. So, something that happened in the past has an impact right now.'

Q stared at her, as if she were a ghost.

'Think about this sentence: *I have had my breakfast*. And answer my three questions by saying, yes or no,' said N.

'But, I don't… What is happening?'

'*I have had my breakfast*. Am I having breakfast right now?'

'No.'

'Did I finish my breakfast before this conversation?'

'Yes.'

'Am I hungry right now?'

'No.'

'You have answered all three questions correctly. I think you understand the present perfect.'

'Mmm.'

'We use contractions when we talk informally. *I've had breakfast.*'

Q said, 'I know. *You've had breakfast. She's had... They've had... We've had...*'

'Can you make a negative statement using the present perfect?'

'*I haven't had breakfast.*'

'As a question?'

'*Have you had breakfast?*'

N was relieved that Q could form these sentences without her help. She stroked the black petals of a flower.

'We can use adverbs such as *already* and *yet,* when we use the present perfect.'

'I have *already* had my breakfast,' said Q, 'I have not *yet* had my breakfast.'

'There is another use of the present perfect. We use it when we talk about our experiences.'

'*Have you ever been to the Garden of Grammar?*'

'Wonderful example… You are asking me whether I have ever had the experience of being in the Garden of Grammar. It doesn't matter when I was there. What is important is that I had the experience of being there. We can use adverbs such as *ever* and *never* in such sentences. *I have never been to the Garden of Grammar.*'

'I have seen the Grammar Wizard last night.'

Frowning, N shook her head.

'What you just said is grammatically incorrect. Darling, you should have used the past simple. *I saw the Grammar Wizard last night.*'

'Why are you giving me a grammar lesson?'

'I'll tell you why your sentence is wrong. One important thing to know about the present perfect is that it's *unfinished time. Have you had breakfast this morning?* This means that this morning is still continuing. It's *unfinished time.* If it's the evening, and I'm asking about something that happened in the morning, then the morning is *finished time.* So, I should use the past simple. *Did you have breakfast this morning?*'

N glanced at the clock on the wall. It was a quarter to seven o'clock. There was not much time left.

'You do know what the past participle is, don't you?'

'Not sure.'

'It's a form of the verb that usually ends in -ed. Some of the past participles of verbs are the same as their past forms. Tell me some examples.'

'Mmm... For the verb *have*, its past participle is *had*... For *surprise*, it is *surprised*... For *send*, it's *sent*,' said Q.

'There are verbs whose past participle forms are different from their past forms. Examples?'

'I can't think of any right now.'

'For the verb *be*, it's *been*.'

'Okay... And for *go*, it's *gone*... For *eat*, it's *eaten*.'

'Think about everything we have talked about. And tell me the form of the present perfect.'

'*Have* or *has* + *past participle*.'

'Wonderful. The negative form?'

'*Haven't* or *hasn't* + *past participle*.'

'We use contractions only in informal speech. You really have become good at grammar.'

'Like I was telling you N, I've been travelling across the Dimension. My grammar has improved so much because...'

'The present perfect continuous tense...'

'Do we really have to talk about it right now?'

'We use the present perfect continuous to talk about an activity that started in the past, and it has continued till the present.'

In the kitchen, there was a door which led to the backyard. Since the house was in the shape of the letter Q, the backyard was a closed space. From this door, a sound came: peck... peck... peck.

Q glanced at the door.

'Look at me! Here is a sentence in the present perfect continuous. *I have been learning grammar all morning*,' said N.

'Your sentence means I have been learning grammar till now.'

The sound from the door did not stop—peck, peck, peck.

'Tell me a sentence in the present perfect continuous. Now!' said N.

'*I have been waiting to tell you something.*'

'When we use the present perfect continuous, we can use conjunctions such as *since* and *for*. We use *since* to say when something began. I have been waiting to tell you something *since* six o'clock. We use *for* to say how long something has been happening.'

'I've been waiting to tell you something *for* the past twenty minutes.'

'That's a good use of the present perfect continuous with *for*. Remember, we use *since* with a point in time—*since seven o'clock*. And we use *for* with a period of time—*for twenty minutes*.'

Peck...peck...peck.

'Make a negative statement in the present perfect continuous,' said N.

'*I haven't been learning grammar all day.*'

'Use the present perfect continuous in a question.'

'*Have you been keeping something from me?*'

'When we use the present perfect continuous, we can use the phrase: *how long*.'

'*How long have you been keeping something from me?*' asked Q.

'You've got it,' said N, snapping her fingers.

The sound got louder: peck peCK PECK.

'We also use the present perfect continuous to talk about an activity that has just stopped, and we can see its results. *It's been raining*. Look at the rainbow.'

'Mmm... So, there's a rainbow because it was raining,' said Q.

'Say something in the present continuous.'

'I can't...'

'Please. You must try. You must.'

'*I've been travelling for four days.* I'm tired.'

'Wonderful. What's the form for the present perfect continuous?' asked N.

'Have or has + I have no idea.'

'*Have* or *has* + *been* + *ing form of the verb.*'

'Okay!'

PECK, PECK, PECK.

N held the blue vase in her arms close to her chest. The three flowers in it were hopping up and down.

'Do you know what the difference between the present perfect continuous and the present perfect is?'

'N! I'm not interested, right now.'

'We use the present perfect continuous when we want to focus on the duration of an activity. For example, *I have been writing for two hours.* And, we use the present perfect when we want to focus on the result of an activity, when the action is complete. Here's an example: *I have written a short story.*'

PECK! PECK! PECK!

'Somebody has been knocking on our door for more than five minutes!' shouted Q.

The noise was giving him a headache. He rushed to the door and opened it.

'Wakey-wakey!' screamed Woo, the word-pecker.

Its wings flapped wildly in the air.

Q turned around to tell N about Woo. She had vanished. His feet felt lighter. He glanced down to look at his red slippers. He was barefoot.

He was in a room in the Grammar Wizard's cottage. A rhythmic sound came from outside. He went to the window. It was raining. Squinting at the rain, he gasped in surprise. On the window, green and red raindrops trickled down. Farther away, in the garden, large, black raindrops fell from fluffy, black clouds. Suddenly, a shower of blue raindrops hit the window. Q pressed his nose on the glass, taking in the sight.

CHAPTER 10

In the Garden of Grammar: Past and Future Perfect

P and Q met in the corridor. The rain was pattering on the roof. 'I had the strangest dream last night,' said Q.

'I couldn't get much sleep,' said P, 'There is something about this place. I cannot put my finger on it.'

'Do you think we're safe?'

'Yes, of course, I do. But there's something they're hiding from us. Let's go down.'

The Grammar Wizard was sitting in the rocking chair. M was at the table. She was editing a report on how to get energy from the zero article. She thoughtfully crossed out a word.

The Grammar Wizard asked, 'P, have you slept well?'

Q noticed that she had just used the present perfect.

'Yes, I have,' said P.

M placed the pencil on the table.

'Q?'

'I had a dream.'

'What did you dream about?' asked M.

'About home… About my wife… The present perfect tense….'

The Grammar Wizard said, 'Ooh… I just love grammar dreams.'

'I never knew about the present perfect. How could I have dreamt about it?' said Q.

M said, 'Sometimes, the flowers give you a grammar lesson while you sleep.'

She collected her papers and pencils and went into the kitchen. She was upset that the flowers had given Q a grammar dream without her knowledge.

The Grammar Wizard entered the kitchen.

'I didn't ask them to give Q a dream.'

M was crushing some pomegranate seeds in a bowl.

'You mean they did it on their own?'

M poured the pomegranate juice into a jug. Some juice spilled onto the kitchen counter.

'The flowers must have been observing your behaviour. They would have acted like you in the dream,' said the Grammar Wizard, with a slight smile.

'They are becoming quite mischievous.'

'The flowers are trying to help us. They thought Q needed to know about the present perfect. Nothing else to it.'

There was not much conversation at the breakfast table. Q was still trying to make sense of his grammar dream. P kept glancing at the Grammar Wizard's eyebrows.

After breakfast, P and Q sat on the orange sofa. The Grammar Wizard, gazing at a rainbow, was by a window. At the other window, M spoke with a spell-checker owl. The Grammar Wizard returned to her rocking chair.

'Q, life before grammar was terrible. Certain uncountable nouns would disappear for years, making everyone miserable. There were even days when one could not use the present simple tense; many people would become impatient trying to explain things. Word-peckers hardly ever made words. When they did, there were so many spelling errors that the words made no sense at all. This created a lot of confusion in the Dimension. Spell-checker owls were always sad and short-tempered. The garden you are in was a dark and gloomy place. Fortunately, the first Grammar Wizard, with inspiration from the grammatica flowers, wrote the first grammar book. Once everyone agreed on the rules, people could finally understand each other. A whole new world opened for us. We started using articles for our energy needs, and abstract nouns for heating and cooking. In the time of the third Grammar Wizard, we even started to cultivate punctuation marks. There would never be a shortage of hyphens, apostrophes, and full stops.'

Q said, 'Woz told me the time before grammar was really hard.'

The Grammar Wizard said, 'I am glad you spent time with Woz. No one knows the past like he does. Whenever I am in Biblios, I always make it a point to visit the Memory Store. Ooh… I must have filled at least ten memory jars.'

The spell-checker owl flew away. M waved at the bird and closed the window.

'Did the owl have any news for us?' asked the Grammar Wizard.

M replied, 'We spoke about the Word Fields. There is some talk among the word-peckers. They say someone is planning to make anti-grammatical sand.'

The Grammar Wizard crossed her arms and sighed.

'There have been so many rumours about anti-grammatical sand. When will they end?'

'But what is anti-grammatical sand?' asked Q.

'It is poison. It affects all living beings that are sensitive to grammar. If a teaspoon of anti-grammatical sand falls on my skin, I will lose all my grammatical knowledge. Forever!' M replied.

The Grammar Wizard nodded her head.

'It is complicated to make anti-grammatical sand, though. The sand must come from the shores of the Sea of Wishes, which is in the Second Conditional Zone. The sand has to be collected by a bird. I imagine that no sensible bird would dare fly in the Second Conditional Zone. It is far too dangerous. There are stories of birds turning to stone. Then one must have the right spell. It is in a book called *The Grammar of Spells*. No one knows where the book is. We have been searching for it for decades. The spell only works in the third month of the Year of the Dash. That year comes only once in twenty years. And it must be a full moon night.'

P said, 'We're in the Year of the Dash. It's already the end of the second month.'

'I know, I know,' whispered the Grammar Wizard.

Placing his hands behind his back, P paced up and down the room. He stopped near the winding staircase, and he twirled his moustache.

'When I was at the Memory Store, I, by complete accident of course, opened someone's memory jar.'

'By accident, of course,' said the Grammar Wizard.

'By accident… I cannot forget those aromas.'

The Grammar Wizard asked, 'What were they?'

'Wet earth… apples… wood.'

Rocking back and forth, the Grammar Wizard thought about the aromas. *Wet earth… This means it was raining… Wood… Could be anywhere there are trees… Apples… Well, apple trees grow in the north.*

'Is there anything else you could tell us. Was there a label on the jar?'

'The name was blackened out, so I don't know whose jar it was. Fortunately, I was able to read the base emotion of the memory. It was jealousy.'

'A powerful negative abstract noun, indeed. It could make a person do terrible things. Terrible things…', said the Grammar Wizard.

'There was also a description of where the memory was made. It was *somewhere above the clouds*,' said P.

'Somewhere above the clouds,' said the Grammar Wizard, raising her eyebrow on the word *clouds*.

'Somewhere above the clouds,' repeated M, slowly and sadly.

'The only time I've been somewhere above the clouds is when I was at the Circle of Magic Trees,' said Q.

The Grammar Wizard said: 'You make a good point. Twenty years ago, there was a competition for the Lamp of Grammar. The first part of the competition consisted of answering questions from the magic trees. Each tree asked nine questions. Then for the second part of the competition, one had to write an essay on what one would do if one became the Grammar Wizard. While we were writing, it rained heavily. Our essays were soaked with green ink. We could not read a word of what we had written. The magic trees allowed us to use their leaves to re-write our essays. Before we started to write again, the magic tree representing verbs told each of us to have an apple. My apple gave me the energy to complete my essay.'

P said, 'It explains all the three aromas in the memory jar. How many candidates were there?'

'Let me think… Ah, yes, there were seven of us.'

'Then we need to interview the other six people. Maybe one of them could tell us something,' said P.

The Grammar Wizard said, 'There may be no time to interview all of them. I am certain we are going to meet one of those six people very soon. Q will have to face this person—this person who is full of jealousy.'

'Why does it have to be me? What do I have to do with any of this? Last night, I dreamt about my home and my wife. I'm going back to Alphabet Village. Today is the end of my journey. No more exploring for me. End of story.'

'Perhaps you should spend some time in the garden with M,' said the Grammar Wizard.

M and Q walked on a muddy path. They saw Ha under a tree. He was dipping a quill pen into a stream of blue ink. A quill pen is a writing instrument made from a feather. Ha's quill pen was a birthday gift from a spell-checker owl.

Ha looked up when he heard their squishy footsteps.

'How are you, my dear Q?'

'All of you can find someone else. Please find someone who really understands grammar. I don't understand what is happening. I don't understand why it has to be me. I want to leave.'

'How could you be so upset? You have an opportunity to serve the Grammar Wizard. It is a privilege. Why don't you have a chat with M? You will feel better after that. Trust me.'

Ha winked at M. She rolled her eyes at him. Q and M walked on a path, with blue and black grammatica flowers on both sides. When Q passed the flowers, their petals closed in a bit.

'M, why do these flowers close?'

'Grammatica flowers are able to sense how much grammar you know. If you know grammar really well, they open up fully. If it is a little less, they close a bit. Less than that, they close some more. If you don't know any grammar at all, they close shut.'

'I can't wait to tell my wife about all of this. She loves grammar.'

'Do you miss her?'

'I do. For the past few months, she hasn't been spending much time at home. She's always been busy with her book club meetings. She's such a bookworm.'

'Mmm.'

They sat on a bench and saw streams of ink trickling down the four mountains. The snow on each mountain top was in a different colour—red, black, blue, and green.

'Maybe, she has her reasons. Isn't this a beautiful place to talk about grammar?' said M.

'Another lesson?'

'Since you have already dreamt about the present perfect tense, I'll talk about the past perfect tense. Here's an example: *I had finished reading my book when the book talk started.*'

'This is something my wife would say. So, you had completed the book before the talk started.'

'Yes. We use the past perfect to talk about something that happened in the past before something else that happened in the past. What's the form of the past perfect?'

'*Had + past participle.*'

'Wonderful! See the flowers around you,' said M.

The red petals of some nearby flowers opened a bit.

'I want the flowers to be in full bloom, like they are around you,' said Q.

'Patience. You'll get there. I'll talk a little about the past perfect continuous tense. Can you guess what it is?'

'It's about two activities in the past. And one activity was continuous.'

'You're on the right path. We use the past perfect continuous to talk about an activity that went on over a period of time till a past moment or stopped just before it.'

'I'm confused.'

'*When the word-peckers arrived, I had been writing in my diary,*' said M.

'Ahhh... So, you were doing something before the word-peckers arrived. You were writing, and it was a continuous action.'

'Yes. We often use the past perfect continuous when we want to stress on the duration of an activity. Make a sentence using this tense.'

'*When my friends arrived, I had been cooking for thirty minutes.*'

Snapping her fingers, M smiled in the direction of the Dimension Mountains.

'And before you ask me what the form is, I'll tell you: *had been + ing form of the verb,*' said Q.

'I'm impressed. Do you know why I'm teaching you all this grammar?'

'Why is everyone I meet so eager to give me a grammar lesson?'

'The third Grammar Wizard wrote that someone, who is not on the Grammar Council, will save the Grammar Dimension from days of darkness. The person will have a good heart, but he or she may not know grammar very well. When our Grammar Wizard read your article, she was convinced that you were the one. All the spell-checker owls agreed with her.'

Q's jaw dropped.

'You created your destiny,' said M, stressing each word.

She watched him closely to see how he was taking the news.

'My wife would be surprised to hear you. She always complains that I never pay enough attention to my grammar,' said Q.

M mumbled, 'She would be absolutely shocked.'

Q gazed at a mountain top. It was covered in red snow, which sparkled in the sunlight.

'I never asked for this. The idea for my article just came to me. I never thought it would be read by so many people. Anyways, I must go back to tell my wife what is happening.'

'I understand you need some time to think about all of this. As for your wife, you can send her a postcard via a spell-checker owl.'

'Thanks.'

Q reluctantly took out his notebook. He made some notes on the past perfect and the past perfect continuous.

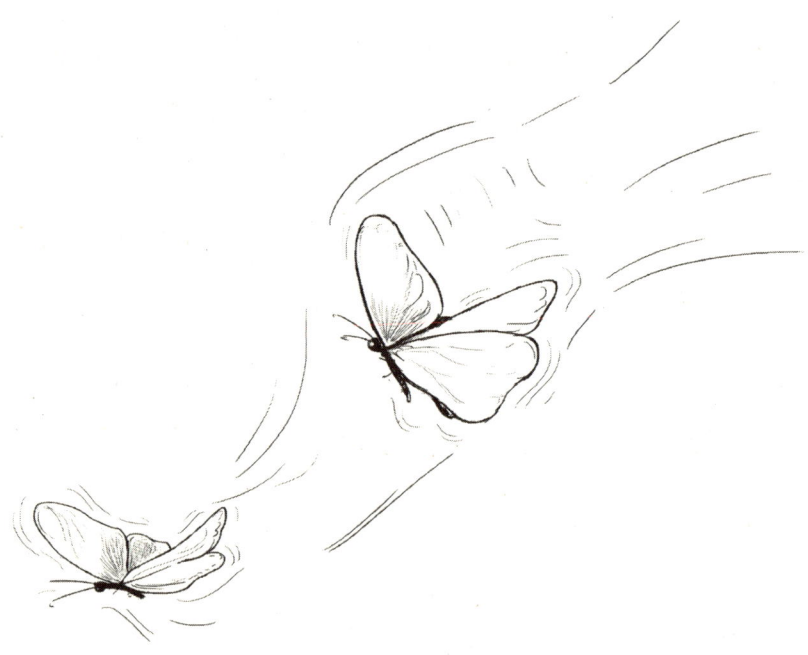

Two yellow butterflies fluttered by; they were chasing each other. One butterfly settled on a petal of a red flower while, the other flew in circles.

'Before we leave, I should tell you something else,' said M.

'Tell me.'

'We must talk about the future perfect tense. The future perfect is used to talk about something that we think will be completed by a particular time in the future.'

'Hmm... And I thought you'll tell me a secret. Okay. Let me try to make a sentence in the future perfect. *I will have learnt about the future perfect before noon*,' said Q.

'Yes. Don't be so sure of yourself. It never helps when you're learning grammar. Can you tell me the form?'

Q scribbled: *will have + past participle.*

With some difficulty, M read his writing.

'You've got it right. Let's get back to the cottage. Oh. Do you want to write that postcard? I've got one here.'

She took out a postcard from her pocket and unfolded it. On one side, there was a painting of a green grammatica flower.

Holding the postcard, Q touched the stem of the painted flower.

'You remind me a lot of my wife. Her name is N. It's the way you explain grammar points. The words you use...'

He glanced at the two dots on her chin.

'It's just a coincidence. What else can it be? Please write a message,' said M.

She glared at a red grammatica flower. A fat drop of blue ink slid down its leaf.

Q wrote two sentences on the card and handed it over to M. She held it tightly.

They walked towards the cottage.

'Just a coincidence… Do you honestly think so? I think there's more to it than that. I think you know more about my grammar dream than you're telling me. Did you ask the flowers to give me the dream? Everything here is so strange and at the same time, so familiar. I think that…,' said Q

She shouted, 'Ha!'

'I think you know everything about me and everything about P. I can feel it when you speak to me. Where did we meet? Was it in Biblios? Did someone tell you about me, about P? Why can't you tell us the truth? Wow spoke about anti-grammatical forces. Is that why? You know we would never do anything to harm the Dimension. P has been in the service of the Grammar Wizard for years. And I would never ever… And still… Don't you trust us? What are you hiding? Ever since we came to the garden, you've been…'

Before he could say another word, Ha appeared.

'There you are. Could you please tell Q about the future perfect continuous tense?' asked M.

'How is the Garden of Grammar?' asked Ha.

'I love it here. But, I feel there's something all of you are hiding from me. I can see it in your eyes. Why don't you tell me the truth?'

'I do not know what you are talking about. We want what is best for you,' said Ha.

'I know you won't harm me,' said Q, 'But still.'

'Then all I ask you to do is to trust us for a little longer. Please…,' said M.

'For a little while longer.'

'Let's talk about something I do know about. The future perfect continuous tense. *By six o'clock this evening, I will have been painting for three hours*,' said Ha.

'Mmm... We're talking about an activity which will have been going on till six o'clock. Is that it?'

'Yes. We use the future perfect continuous to emphasise how long something will have been going on till a particular time in the future,' said Ha.

'By this Friday, I will have been travelling in the Grammar Dimension for five days.'

'When you said, *"five days"* you were highlighting the number of days you have been travelling for.'

'And now you will ask me what the form of the future perfect continuous is.'

'And it is,' said Ha, raising his right hand dramatically.

Q thought for a while. He wrote—*will have been + ing form of the verb.*

'You are correct,' said Ha.

They walked towards the Dimension Mountain Range. Q saw that the flowers near Ha were in full bloom.

'This is a magical place. I never dreamed it would be like this. When I came here, I was upset, but now, I feel so calm. Can I pluck a flower for my wife?' said Q.

'She would like that. I am sure of it,' said Ha.

Q kneeled and gently plucked a black grammatica flower.

'I'll ask a spell-checker owl to give it to her, along with your postcard,' said M.

M wanted to speak with the flowers. She wanted to question them about Q's grammar dream. Unfortunately, she could not think of an excuse to get away from Q and Ha. And Q was already getting suspicious.

They were at the foothills of the mountains. Ha told the story of how the rules of grammar were made:

The first Grammar Wizard used to spend a lot of time admiring grammatica flowers. Once, in a dream, the eight petals of the flower inspired him to discover the eight parts of speech. He travelled everywhere in the Dimension to learn more about how grammar works. He searched for the Circle of Magic Trees. He built the first towers at the Articles Station. He even tried to grow commas, but that did not work out well. He spent years in the Third Conditional Zone. Wherever he went, he always carried a lamp. He used to write late into the night in the light of that lamp. Over time, the lamp came to be known as the Lamp of Grammar. It is with us today. And it is given to the person who becomes the new Grammar Wizard.

After listening to Ha's story, M said that they should return to the cottage.

Ha went to his tree. His quill pen was peeking out of his notebook. He was writing a script for a play set in a time before grammar. It was a play about three word-peckers that could not agree on where to go.

M and Q entered the cottage. The Grammar Wizard, sitting at the round table, was unrolling an old map of the Dimension. P stood near the bookcase. He was sipping a mixture of red and blue ink.

'Welcome back! Q, I see you have a flower in your hand. Lovely... M can find a vase for it. Why don't both of you join us?' said the Grammar Wizard.

The map of the Dimension was roughly in the shape of a rectangle. The Dimension was surrounded by the Ocean of Ink. What was beyond it was a mystery: no living being had ever crossed it.

In the east of the Dimension, was the Garden of Grammar. Above the garden, there was the Dimension Mountain Range. The four rivers of ink flowed from this mountain range. The rivers flowed through the Dimension, giving it life.

The River of Blue Ink, the longest of all the rivers, flowed west. Alphabet Village was on this river.

The River of Black Ink flowed southwest. It flowed through the Word Fields and the Punctuation Grove.

The River of Red Ink, the shortest of all the rivers, flowed south. It was a fast-moving river with many boulders in it.

The River of Green ink flowed north. It went through the Conditional Zones and through the town of Biblios.

In the northeast part of the map, there was a large circle. It was labelled: *zero*. Inside the *zero* circle, there was a circle. It was labelled: *first*. Inside the *first* circle, there was a circle. It was labelled: *second*. Inside the *second* circle, there was a circle. It was labelled: *third*. The *third* circle was just a dot.

'What does *zero* mean?' asked Q.

The Grammar Wizard replied, in a grave tone, 'All these circles represent the Conditional Zones.'

'I have been there many times,' said P. 'If one is not careful, one could get stuck there for a long time.'

'Well, I hope we're not going there,' said Q.

The Grammar Wizard looked at Q and then at P.

'Actually, it is your next destination,' she said.

'As long as we will not be in the Third Conditional Zone, we should be safe.' said P. 'I'm not fond of that zone. It is such a depressing place.'

'It is exactly where you need to go. There is a powerful grammar potion that will help Q. Grammar Potion Number 9 is made in that zone, and nowhere else,' said the Grammar Wizard.

'Come on, P. We've controlled a negative abstract noun leak. How hard could it be to find a potion?' said Q.

M whispered to the flower in her hand, 'He doesn't have a clue about the conditionals.'

At the top of the staircase, a word-pecker was listening to all that was being discussed below. When the bird heard enough, it quietly flew out through an open window.

CHAPTER 11

The Zero and First Conditional Zones

In the Grammar Dimension there are four conditional zones: the Zero Conditional Zone, the First Conditional Zone, the Second Conditional Zone, and the Third Conditional Zone. P and Q have to go to the Third Conditional Zone to get Grammar Potion Number 9. Each zone, except the Zero Conditional Zone, is surrounded by another zone. The Third Conditional Zone can only be reached by crossing all the other zones.

They had left the garden and were flying above the River of Green Ink. Q was already missing the gentle grammatica flowers.

'How far is the Zero Conditional Zone?'

'If the wind remains at this speed, we should be there before evening,' P replied.

'It's dangerous to fly over the Zero Conditional Zone, isn't it?'

'It's safe. However, we can't travel by balloon over the First Conditional Zone. The winds always change direction there. We could lose control. Worse things happen in the other two zones.'

'And what is it like in the Zero Conditional Zone?'

'The people are honest and hardworking. They tend to speak frankly. I like them very much.'

Q had time to catch up on his notes on the present, past, and future perfect.

The balloon floated into the clear sky of the Zero Conditional Zone. It landed near a group of seven houses. In one house, smoke rose from its chimney. A man peered through a window. Grabbing his straw hat, he came out to greet them.

'P! So good to see you. What brings you to our zone?'

'I'd like to keep this balloon here for a few days. Would it be alright, Pil?'

'Are you, by any chance, going to the Second Conditional Zone?'

'In fact, we are headed for the Third Conditional Zone. We are on a mission for the Grammar Wizard.'

Pil bit his upper lip.

'What happens in the Third Conditional Zone?' asked Q.

'One conditional zone at a time. Right now, we're in the Zero Conditional Zone. Pil, could you tell Q about the zero conditional?' said P.

'Yup. I invite you to my home. There's some ink on the stove. We can talk about the zero conditional over hot chocolate.'

Pil asked them to make themselves comfortable in his living room. Old weather-beaten books were stacked along a wall. The bubbling sound of boiling ink came from the kitchen. Q warmed his hands by the fireplace. P skimmed through a book on how to take care of apostrophe trees.

Pil was in the kitchen. He poured the hot, green ink from the kettle into three mugs. He put a generous spoonful of chocolate powder into each mug. Using a spoon, he mixed the chocolate powder with the ink. He placed the mugs on a wooden tray and served his guests. He sat down in a chair.

Drumming his fingers on the table, Pil blew into his mug of hot chocolate.

'What do you know about the zero conditional?'

'Not much,' Q replied.

'The zero conditional is all about something that is believed to be factually true. We use it for a scientific fact. We are sure of what the result will be. *If snow melts, it becomes ink.*'

'*If you freeze ink, it becomes ice,*' said Q.

'Yup, that's the zero conditional as well.'

'Do we use the zero conditional to talk about the future?'

'No, the zero conditional doesn't refer to any time period.'

'And the form of the zero conditional is: *if + present simple, present simple.*'

Pil muttered, 'Why do all these young people ask for the form? You want everything to be so easy nowadays.'

'It helps me to make other sentences in the zero conditional.'

'Yup, the form you said is right. You can also use the word *when* instead of *if.*'

'*When you freeze ink, it becomes ice,*' said Q.

The steam from the hot chocolate fogged Pil's steel-rimmed spectacles. He removed them and held them in his hands.

'P, why do you have to go to the Second Conditional Zone? Why?'

'As I said, we are on a mission for the Grammar Wizard. We have to go to the Third Conditional Zone to find a grammar potion.'

'I don't believe in any grammar potions. You improve your knowledge of grammar by reading good books, not by drinking some silly potion. Simple as that.'

'What can I say, Pil? We are following the instructions of the Grammar Wizard,' said P.

'Does Q know the dangers of the Second Conditional Zone?' asked Pil.

'I haven't told him yet. Why don't you?'

Pil said, 'Be careful when you are in the Second Conditional Zone. You must control your thoughts. When you're there, your thoughts come alive. If you wish for something, it becomes reality. Well, your wishes don't always come true. They come true when the stars stop dancing and form a punctuation mark. No one can predict when it happens.'

'The stars dance!' said Q.

'They move around in circles, up and down. That kind of thing... You'll see when you get there,' said Pil, putting his spectacles back on.

'If your wishes come true, why doesn't everyone live there?'

'Once your wish becomes reality, it's difficult to take it back,' said Pil, 'I have friends who have lost their minds in the Second Conditional Zone. Be very careful.'

'Listen, not everyone has gone crazy. I know many poets and painters who enjoy living there,' said P.

Q saw the bubbles pop in his mug of hot chocolate. He hoped he would survive the Second Conditional Zone.

'Walk with us till the green door,' said P. 'I haven't seen you for such a long time.'

Pil reached for his straw hat.

They crossed the fields of golden stalks of corn, swaying gently in the breeze. Pil took long strides as he walked. P and Q had to quicken their pace to keep up with him.

'What's that?' asked Q.

It was a thick clay wall which curved slightly inwards.

'That's the boundary between the Zero and the First Conditional Zone,' Pil said. 'What do you know about the first conditional?'

'Zero,' replied Q.

'Do you mind P if we spend a few minutes here before entering the next zone?' Pil asked.

'No, I don't. Please hurry. We're on a mission for the Grammar Wizard.'

'I've always admired P. He is so dedicated to his job. Did you know P is the most decorated officer in the history of the Dimension?' said Pil.

'He never told me.'

'That's another thing I like about him. He's always modest. Are you ready to learn about the first conditional?'

Q placed his notebook on the side of the smooth wall.

'The first conditional is all about things that are likely to happen in the future. *If you work hard, you will succeed*,' said Pil.

'Let me try to make a sentence,' said Q. '*If you read lots of books, your grammar will improve*.'

'That's the way I learned my grammar. The only way.'

'What's the form?'

'There you go again asking about the form. Why, it's right in front of you. Look!'

Q ran his fingers over the first conditional sentences written in his notebook.

He wrote: *if + present simple, will + infinitive without to*

'Yup. There you go. That's your form,' said Pil, pushing open the gate.

Q was the first to enter the First Conditional Zone. The only difference in this zone was that the stalks of corn stood still. Suddenly, a gust of wind blew through the field.

'This looks exactly the same as the Zero Conditional Zone,' said Q.

Pil removed his hat. He bent down to pass through the gate.

'These are sensible zones. It's the second and third ones that don't make any sense. Those are the unreal zones.'

Q said, 'Maybe, we should stay in these zones.'

'Tell me. How is your wife?' Pil asked P.

'X's as busy as ever—still in charge of the branch library near our house. She also organises book talks across the Dimension.'

'I met X when she came here to give a talk on how to read a history book,' said Pil.

'I remember she told me she had met you. Anything unusual happened here?'

'Well, just this morning I saw a word-pecker flying very low over my fields in the First Conditional Zone.'

'I thought birds avoid this zone. The air currents change direction all the time here. A few years ago, two spell-checker owls crashed into each other,' said P.

'What's strange is that the word-pecker seemed to be flying from where the green door is located.'

'You mean it could have been coming from the Second Conditional Zone. Now, that is strange. Horrible things happen to word-peckers in that zone.'

'I really don't know what the word-pecker was thinking,' said Pil.

'Is there anything else you'd like to tell Q about the first conditional?' asked P.

'Yup, there is. When we have a sentence in the first conditional, the conditional clause can come at the beginning or the end of the sentence.'

'If you work hard, you will succeed. You will succeed if you work hard,' said Q.

'Yup. And when you write, if the conditional clause comes first, you put a comma after it.'

They reached the door, it was a green door in the middle of a cornfield. Pil removed his hat and twisted its rim.

'Q, I wish you luck.'

P opened the door. He nudged Q into the Second Conditional Zone.

CHAPTER 12

The Second Conditional Zone

Two bright stars chased each other across the night sky, just like two butterflies fluttering in a garden. One star spiralled up and the other spiralled down. Seven stars swung back and forth, as if they were sitting on swings. Groups of stars formed triangles, squares, and circles. And these triangles, squares, and circles were moving in all directions. Only the full moon stayed in its place. Q gaped at the spectacle.

'Stay where you are!' said P.

'The stars...' said Q.

'I will never forget the night when the stars came together to form a punctuation mark.'

'And what did they form?'

'A question mark. It was simply brilliant. I blinked and it was gone.'

'I hope to see something like that.'

'Be careful what you wish for, especially when wishes can come true.'

'I suppose so.'

'I don't see any boats. We'll have to swim to the other side.'

Q heard the rumbling sound of waves. They were by the Sea of Wishes. With the help of the moonlight, he could make out a shoreline in the distance.

'But… but… P, I can't swim. How can I get there?'

P took out a metallic box from his pocket. It opened with a click.

'Take this pill. Repeat what I say, and you will be able to swim to the other side. Understood?'

There were four pink pills in the box. P selected one and gave it to Q.

'When you swim, just follow the reflection of the moon. It will lead you straight to the shore. Don't stop. Keep moving forward,' said P.

'How can I swim?'

'Swallow the pill. Repeat after me.'

It was easy to swallow the pill. It was only a little larger than any of the full stops on this page.

P said, '*If I were a fish, I would swim to the other side.*'

'*If I were a fish, I would swim to the other side.*'

'Jump!'

Splash. Splash. They were in the salty ink.

Q shivered in the cold liquid. He wrapped his arms around his chest. His legs felt funny. They were pressing against each other with a lot of force. Turning his head sideways, he saw ink all around him. A blanket of silvery light floated above him.

What is happening? Am I drowning?

He stretched his hands to touch the light, but he could not reach it.

Have my hands shrunk?

He swam up towards the dancing stars. He now understood that the blanket of silvery light was the reflection of the moon on the surface of the sea. Q opened his mouth in amazement—bubbles tumbled out. Through the bubbles he saw something dark that was moving in the ink.

It must be P.

He turned his head to the left. Something long, like a fat fountain pen, was gliding towards him.

What's a pen doing swimming around in ink?

The pen came closer to him. He could now clearly make out a triangle attached to it.

It's a shark. Ahhh!

Q's body effortlessly weaved through the ink. He swam as fast as he could. However fast he managed to go, the shark's cold eyes remained close by.

Q swam to the white foam of a wave and was carried ashore. He gasped for breath. His tail slapped the sand. From the corner of his eye, he saw the shark. It had followed him onto the beach. The shark opened its mouth wide, displaying a set of razor-sharp teeth. The teeth were only a few centimetres away from Q.

Q lay helplessly on the beach. A few grains of sand were in his mouth. He used his hand to remove the sand from his tongue. He brought his hand in front of him, spreading his fingers wide.

'My hands!'

He touched his hair, his nose, and his toes.

P was laughing so much that there were tears streaming down his cheeks.

Q screamed, 'You were the shark!'

'Yes, I was. I've never had so much fun in my life.'

'I thought I was going to be eaten.'

'When you made your wish to become a fish, you could have chosen to turn into any kind of fish. You thought of a goldfish. Those goldfish in the Pools of the Present have left a strong impression on you. I thought of a shark; I became one.'

'How could you?' asked Q.

'It was the only way to get you moving. Otherwise, you would have spent the whole night discovering what it was like to be a goldfish. The effects of the pill don't last for long. I had to get you to the other side as quickly as possible.'

'Next time, I'll be prepared.'

Peering into the darkness, P chuckled.

'I'm always in for a surprise when I visit this zone.'

'What is it? Is it a town?'

'Oh, I think I know what it is.'

They went to the structure. It now looked like a very large building. P pulled a green rope which rang the bell. After twenty minutes, a woman, holding a lantern, opened the door. The light from the lantern illuminated her sad, tired eyes.

'May I help you?' she asked.

'Good evening. My friend and I have just come from the First Conditional Zone. We are searching for a place to rest. May we stay here for the night?' said P.

'Please come in.'

P and Q dripped green ink onto the marble floor.

'Oh my, oh my! You'll need some towels. Please go to the twenty-first bedroom on your right. The rooms are past the two drawing rooms and the studio with all my paintings. It's a bit of a walk. I know... There are some towels in the closet. There are some clothes there as well. They should fit you. And oh... My name is Cleo.'

'Thank you, Cleo. My name is P. This is Q.'

'You've come just in time for dinner. I'll take... umm... thirty minutes to bring the food. The kitchen is so far away.'

They went through two spacious living rooms that had sofas and chairs and tables. They entered the studio that had Cleo's paintings. Some of her paintings were hung on the wall. And many were on the floor, leaning against the wall. All the paintings were of the sky. Some were of the sky filled with green clouds. But most of the paintings were of the sky at night, with the dancing stars.

They spent a few minutes admiring the paintings before heading into a hallway. They walked down the hallway and finally reached the twenty-first room.

After changing into fresh clothes, P flopped onto the bed.

'I'm really getting too old for the Second Conditional Zone.'

They returned to the dining room. There was a long table which could seat all the residents of Alphabet Village. The eight magic trees were painted on a wall. It was a life-size painting of all of them. P thought that if there were a breeze, these trees would speak to him.

'Now is a good time as any to talk about the second conditional,' said P.

'Mmm… I think it has something to do with turning into a goldfish.'

'The second conditional is used when talking about an unreal or impossible situation.'

'*If I were a fish, I would swim to the other side.* It's in the second conditional, right?'

'Yes. In the normal world, you could never turn into a fish. You can try when we get back.'

Q said, '*If I were a bookworm, I would eat lots of words.*'

'Very good. Between you and me, I know what has happened here. Someone has wished for something using the second conditional.'

'I remember Pil telling me I need to be careful in this zone.'

'It's good advice. Let's finish talking about the second conditional. We often use the verb *were* when we talk in the second conditional. However, we can use other verbs as well.'

'*If I knew grammar, I would not be in the Second Conditional Zone.*'

'Excellent! You're full of surprises. What's the form of the second conditional?'

Q found a page in his notebook that was not too wet. He jotted down the sentences:

If I were a bookworm, I would eat lots of words.

If I knew grammar, I would not be in the Second Conditional Zone.

He wrote: *if + past simple, would + infinitive without to.*

'I suppose both these sentences are right. *If I were a bookworm, I would eat lots of words. I would eat lots of words if I were a bookworm,*' said Q.

'Correct. You can change the order of the conditional and result clauses,' said P. 'Just remember when the conditional clause comes first….'

'I put a comma after it. I know.'

Q read the sentence: *If I knew grammar, I would not be in the Second Conditional Zone.*

'Here, I have the verb *knew*. Does it mean that when I use the second conditional, I'm talking about the past?'

'Not at all... When we use the second conditional, we are talking about an unreal or impossible situation in the present or the future. We are not talking about the past.'

Cleo brought some food on a trolley. She set three plates at the end of the table. With a big spoon she served them some boiled vegetables and potatoes.

'I hope the food is alright. I haven't been myself lately.'

'It is delicious,' said P.

Cleo ate a spoonful of green beans. She pushed her plate away.

'My husband has always had big dreams. We moved to this zone to have a better life. The soil here is so rich. With a little hard work, you can grow anything.'

The food grown in this zone was known to be quite tasty.

'Every evening, after he came back from work, my husband would say: *If I were a rich man, we would live in a house with ten thousand rooms.*'

'The second conditional,' mumbled Q, as he cut through a sweet potato.

P placed his spoon on his plate.

'What happened?'

'Yesterday, after he finished his work, he said the same thing. You know, about the big house...'

'And then all of this appeared out of thin air,' said P, waving his left hand.

'I was in our living room. We had only three rooms before. Suddenly, I found myself in this never-ending mansion. I think my husband was in the bedroom at the time. But there are ten thousand rooms! I've been searching for him since last night.'

P thought hard about how he could help. He knew what had happened. That night, for just a few seconds, the stars came together to form a punctuation mark. Her husband would have made his wish at that exact moment.

Cleo said, 'By the way, how come you two were so wet? You couldn't have swum across the sea. The ferry service is only on Wednesdays.'

P said, 'We'll tell you tomorrow. It's a long story.'

Gazing at her half-eaten plate, she mumbled, Good night.'

She picked up the lantern to carry on the search for her husband.

In another part of the Dimension, in the town of Biblios, the sun was beginning to set.

K, the Grand Librarian, was at his desk. He gazed for a while at a blank page, thinking about how he should present his ideas. He picked up his quill pen and dipped it into a pot of red ink.

It was a letter to his colleagues on the Grammar Council. K wrote that there was an urgent need to look at how words were spelt. There were many words which had confusing spellings. K wanted to simplify spelling, so that one could spell a word just the way it sounds. The quill pen made a scratching sound as he wrote paragraph after paragraph. When he was halfway through his letter, he lit the thick candles that were on his desk. K went back to work, and he finished the letter. After carefully folding it, he placed it in a drawer.

He said to the empty room, 'Ah! If I were the Grammar Wizard, I would be so happy.'

Wrrr! Wrrr!

Glancing at an open window, K shouted, 'Come in, my loyal bird.'

A word-pecker glided in and landed on a pile of books. The flames from the candles flickered.

'Did you bring it?' asked K.

The word-pecker's claws let go of a brown pouch. K rubbed his hands together. He untied the string and thrust his fingers into the pouch.

'The sand from the shores of the Sea of Wishes,' he said. 'Did you have any trouble getting it?'

'No trouble... Wrr... I were flying low when I were over the Conditional Zones. I drunk lots of red ink,' said the word-pecker.

'Excellent... You did exactly what I told you to. Now, what news from the cottage?'

'They thinks it must be somebody who were at the grammar competition with the magic trees. Wrr... P want to meet all the people who was there.'

'Woo. My ears burn when I hear your atrocious grammar. No wonder you were not allowed to work in the Word Fields. I have no idea how the Grammar Wizard puts up with your grammar. About the Circle of Magic Trees... What you say is interesting. They think it is someone who participated in the competition for the Lamp of Grammar. How did they arrive at this conclusion? Oh well, never mind. It doesn't matter now.'

K felt some grains of sand under his fingernails. He washed his hands in a bowl of warm, green ink. After inspecting his fingers using a magnifying glass, he washed his hands again.

'What about Q from Alphabet Village? Is he any good at grammar?'

'Wrr... I thinks he are bad at grammar. I thinks the flowers was giving him a grammar dream.'

'Those nosy flowers. Why don't they mind their own business?'

'I tries to wake him up before his dream ending. Wrrr... Wrrr...'

'You are a useful word-pecker. It is almost time.'

A puddle of wax had formed on the table. The candles were about to burn themselves out. Holding a lantern in one hand, K left his office in a hurry. Woo flapped around him. They went through a maze of quiet passageways.

K took out a big, rusty key and unlocked a door. It creaked open.

'Welcome to the Spelling Room! When all this is over, I shall reward you.'

It was a hexagonal-shaped room full of books. A grandfather clock was next to a window, which was covered by a thin, blue curtain. In the centre of the room, there was a pink marble table.

Using his long sleeves, K brushed away the layer of dust on the table. He placed the pouch of sand on it. He turned his attention to the bookshelves around him. His long fingers ran over the titles printed on the spines of the books. They had titles such as: *How Spell-Checker Owls Learn to Spell* and *Spelling Bee Champions.*

'You see my dear word-pecker, the Spelling Room is a room that stores books on spelling. Last summer, I found a book which I had been searching for years. It was in this room, right under my very nose. Ah... Here it is, *The Grammar of Spells*,' said K.

It was a bulky book with its title written in gold. He placed the book on the table. K peered at the curtain. A smug smile appeared on his face.

'A full moon night, just as the spell-checker owls predicted. Woo, open the window.'

The word-pecker used its beak to draw the curtains and open the window. The pink marble table glowed in the moonlight. Woo perched on top of the grandfather clock.

K read from *The Grammar of Spells*:

Anti-grammatical sand is made at nine o'clock, on a full moon night, in the third month of the Year of the Dash. Contact with anti-grammatical sand may lead to severe memory loss of grammar. Are you sure you know what you are doing?

'Of course, I do. What a pointless question.'

Dong! Dong! Dong!

The grandfather clock shook, causing the word-pecker to topple onto the top of a bookcase.

Dong! Dong! Dong! Dong! Dong! Dong!

As the bells of the grandfather clock rang, K chanted a spell from the book:

This is the spell of bad grammar
which I cast on this sand
from the shores of
the Sea of Wishes.
May we use the article a in front of a vowel sound;
May we end an uncountable noun with the letter s;
May we confuse the past perfect with the past simple;
May we use no punctuation marks in our writing;
May our sentences make no sense at all!
May this sand become ANTI-GRAMMATICAL SAND!

A crackling sound came from the pouch: the sand was reacting to the spell. K put on a pair of white gloves. After the sound stopped, he opened the pouch. The sand's colour was now paper-clip silver.

K sighed with relief.

'Woo, fly to the garden at once. Hide the sand in the cottage. Wait for me.'

The word-pecker landed on the table. Its wings trembled.

'Don't be so scared. Your grammar is so bad that this sand will have no effect on you,' K said.

He slid *The Grammar of Spells* into its place on the bookshelf.

'Wrr... Will the Grammar Wizard knows there are sand in the cottage?'

'No. This is the beauty of anti-grammatical sand. It has no odour. No one will know. Just make sure it stays in the pouch.'

A soft sound came from somewhere close by. Bump.

'Is anyone here?' growled K.

The word-pecker flew to the top of the grandfather clock. It looked at the books, the door, the marble table, and the open window. There was nothing else there.

'I sees no one.'

'Must be the wind on the window.'

'You is right.'

'I shall call for you when I am at the cottage.'

The word-pecker flew over the homes of Biblios. In its claws was a pouch of silvery sand. K locked the door from the outside. He turned the key twice, just to make sure that no one could get in.

* * *

Earlier that day, late in the afternoon, a bookworm named Wow squeezed through the door's keyhole. When K and Woo entered the room, the bookworm was napping in a book titled: *Words with Silent Letters*. It had eaten three words (*knock*, *write*, and *listen*) with silent letters in them. It woke up when it heard the words 'anti-grammatical sand'.

Wow thought: *I wanted to stay still, but I couldn't control myself. I have never heard K speak like this. What is he planning to do? Did he really make anti-grammatical sand?*

If you were Wow, what would you do?

CHAPTER 13

The Third Conditional Zone

Dear Cleo,

Thank you for everything. We need to be at the Third Conditional Slide by this evening. Hope you find your husband soon.

P & Q

P left the note on the dining table. While he was waiting for Q to get ready, he studied the painting of the Circle of Magic Trees. He wanted to touch the thin branches of the tree representing conjunctions, but the paint was still wet.

'Why do you want to go there?' asked Cleo, waving the note in her hand.

She had not slept a wink last night, yet she still spoke with some energy.

'We are on a mission for the Grammar Wizard. We have to meet someone there,' replied P.

'Oooh. Sounds important. You must eat something before you go. I know a short-cut to the slide. You'll be there in good time. I'll be back in half an hour.'

Q entered the dining room.

'Shall we go?'

'Cleo knows a short-cut. We can have breakfast and still make it on time.'

'Why does the food taste so good?' asked Q, patting his belly.

A man stumbled into the room. He tripped on the edge of the carpet and fell. He crawled towards the table. P rushed to help him.

'Excuse me, ehh... have you seen ehh... my wife? Cleo. Cleo...,' mumbled the man.

P said, 'Yes, of course we have. She's in the kitchen.'

'The kitchen... I've ehh... never been there. I've been wandering ehh... bedroom to bedroom... reading room to ehh...'

'Please have a seat,' said P. 'You need ink.'

The man slumped into the chair and gulped down some green ink. His eyelids drooped. Soon, he was fast asleep.

'Darling!' said Cleo.

The man did not hear her. Cleo hugged him.

'Where have you been?' she asked.

'I was ehh… searching for you on ehh… fifth floor.'

'I never made it past the third floor,' said Cleo.

'Next time ehh… I'll be… ehh… careful when I ehh… use the second conditional. I ehh… promise.'

They ate a hearty breakfast. Cleo kept talking about the different rooms in the new house. She said it would be impossible to clean all of them. Finally, she and her husband decided to live in five rooms on the ground floor.

Cleo said bye to her new friends from her porch.

'Stop by on your way back,' she said.

P and Q walked for many hours. They passed rows and rows of peach trees.

'Tell me about the Third Conditional Zone,' asked Q. 'And is there a fourth conditional zone?'

'Don't worry. There is no fourth conditional zone.'

P plucked two peaches and tossed one to Q. A gust of wind made him miss the peach.

'The people who live in the Third Conditional Zone always think about the past. They think about what might have been if things were different,' said P.

'Sounds like they have a lot of regrets.'

'Well, people usually use the third conditional when they regret something that happened in the past.'

They reached the slide which would take them to the Third Conditional Zone. Q imagined the sky in this zone would be grey and cloudy.

'What are we going to do?' asked Q.

P climbed up the ladder and slid down the slide. Swoosh! He disappeared before he reached its end.

'Wait for me!' shouted Q.

As he slid down, he felt the wind pressing on his face. The wind became so strong that it was slowing him down. When he reached the end of the slide, he was surprised. The sun was even brighter here. There were peach trees everywhere.

'To the village,' said P.

They reached the only village in the Third Conditional Zone. There was a board that read: *If we had built twenty-six houses, this village could have been named Alphabet Village.*

Some children were on a stone bridge. They were throwing pebbles into the River of Green Ink. Two villagers were passing Q. He smiled at them, but they looked through him.

P said, 'Most people here are lost in their own thoughts. We must find the person who makes grammar potions.'

They spotted an open-air café. It was on the other side of the bridge. Behind the counter, there was a young man. He ran his fingers through his long frizzy hair and tied it into a ponytail. He whistled a tune while he was boiling some green ink.

'Hello there. People call me R. What would you like to have?'

'We are looking for something to drink,' P replied.

'I can offer you: black coffee, green tea, lemonade, orange juice, apple juice, watermelon juice, and Grammar Potion Number 9.'

'Did you just say Grammar Potion Number 9?' asked P.

'I've enough for two glasses. Would you like some?'

'Yes please,' P replied, trying not to sound too excited.

Grammar Potion Number 9 could only be found in the Third Conditional Zone. There were some people who believed that drinking grammar potions improves one's knowledge of grammar. Then there were others, such as Pil, who were convinced that all this talk of grammar potions was just nonsense.

P and Q sat at a table. They observed how Grammar Potion Number 9 was being made. R bent down, and he plucked five strawberries from a row of strawberry plants. After washing the strawberries, he juggled with them for about thirty seconds, and he tossed them into a wooden bowl. He crushed them with a spoon. He poured half a cup of pomegranate juice into the same bowl. He took out a jar. Q squinted at the label on the jar. It read: Sweet Secret. R sprinkled some Sweet Secret on the juice. What R did next made Q blink twice. R tossed three green ice cubes into an empty glass bowl. The ice cubes floated in the air in the middle of the bowl. Q turned to P for an explanation. P just shrugged his shoulders. R poured the contents of the wooden bowl into the glass bowl with the green ice cubes. He covered the glass bowl with a lid. Holding this bowl above his shoulder, R shook it vigorously back and forth. The grammar potion was poured into two tall glasses.

Two villagers sat at a table behind P and Q.

The first woman said, '*If I had been more organised, I should have finished my book months ago.*'

The second woman said, '*If I had learnt to play the guitar, I would have been a musician.*'

Q whispered to P, 'Are they talking in the third conditional?'

'Everyone here uses the third conditional, all the time. Most visitors to this zone get so used to talking in this conditional that they can't live anywhere else. I never spend much time here.'

The villagers kept on sprinkling their conversation with the third conditional.

'Here you go,' said R, holding two glasses of Grammar Potion Number 9.

'Could I have a glass of lemonade, and an empty flask, please?' asked P.

'If I had known you wanted some lemonade, I could have plucked some lemons,' said R.

Shaking his head, R returned to the counter.

'They really do always use the third conditional,' said Q.

'Why don't you drink a glass of potion? I'll save the rest for later,' said P.

'Is it okay to drink this much potion?' asked Q.

'There are no side effects to grammar potions.'

Q drank some Grammar Potion Number 9. He tried to guess what the secret ingredient was, but he could not identify it.

Glancing around, he said, *'If I had had a place like this in Alphabet Village, I could have opened my own café.'*

'You've started talking in the third conditional. We had better leave soon.'

Q unfolded a fresh napkin and wrote:

Third Conditional

- *We use the third conditional to talk about an imaginary event in the past.*
- *When people regret something they did or did not do in the past, they often express their regret by using the third conditional.*
- *if + past perfect, would have / should have / could have + past participle*

P said, 'The grammar potion is working!'

* * *

K reached the Garden of Grammar by boat. He sailed on the River of Green Ink to get there. It was a hazardous journey because he crossed all the conditional zones.

Sitting by the same river of green ink, Ha was composing a poem on spell-checker owl eggs.

'Ha. How are you?' shouted K.

'Ah! The Grand Librarian. Is there a meeting of the Grammar Council today?'

'No. I have an urgent message for the Grammar Wizard. Is she at the cottage?'

'She is.'

K threw a rope to Ha; Ha pulled the boat ashore. While they were walking towards the cottage, the grammatica flowers, near K, closed shut. He noticed the flowers' strange behaviour. He was excellent at grammar. They should have been in full bloom.

'Are P and Q still here?' asked K.

'They have left for the conditional zones,' said Ha.

'I had the pleasure of meeting Q at the Grand Library,' said K.

'I had a good conversation with him. He is a keen learner,' said Ha.

'Is he? That is good to hear.'

When the cottage came into sight, Ha stopped.

'The magic trees have warned us that the Grammar Wizard is in danger. I am embarrassed to say this. I must make sure you are not carrying anything that may harm her,' said Ha.

'I completely understand. You are, after all, performing your duty.'

K emptied his pockets. He took out a pencil, a notebook, and a pair of white gloves.

'I have this pair of gloves with me because I was reading an old book.'

'No need for explanations. Thank you for being so co-operative. It is just that there are so many rumours going around the Dimension these days. Would you mind if I checked your pockets?'

'I have even heard a rumour that someone is planning to kidnap the Grammar Wizard. I insist you thoroughly check anyone who wishes to see her, including me,' said K.

Ha checked K's pockets to make sure they were empty. He did it quickly.

'How could anyone think of kidnapping the Grammar Wizard?' asked Ha.

'She is a fine grammarian. She has always supported me in the Grammar Council. I cannot imagine anyone wanting to harm her.'

They reached the door of the cottage.

'Well, I leave you here, K. The flowers by the river are calling me. They seem to be worried about something.'

K, the Grand Librarian, knocked on the door. It was opened immediately.

'What a pleasant surprise! Do come in,' said the Grammar Wizard.

She went to the cupboard and picked up an orange teacup that had golden zigzag lines on it.

'Some green tea?'

'There need to be some changes in the Dimension,' said K.

'I know what you mean. When we have our next Grammar Council meeting, you should bring it up. I agree with you. We do need to change the spellings of some words. They have become… mmm… outdated.'

'I am not talking about spelling.'

'Then what are you talking about?'

'If I had answered that last question correctly, I could have won the lamp.'

The Grammar Wizard froze. She remembered what P had said about the memory jar. *The aromas were wet earth, wood, and apples. The competition for the lamp… And K was there.*

'Are you talking about what happened all those years ago?'

'I remember it as if it were yesterday.'

'I thought you were happy being the Grand Librarian. You are doing such wonderful work in Biblios.'

Putting on his gloves, K said, 'There were moments when I enjoyed my work, but I was never happy. I should have been here.'

'We must talk more about this. I have just made some tea. Let's have a ….'

'Woo!' the Grand Librarian yelled.

The word-pecker dived into the room. It dropped the pouch into K's cupped hands.

'Woo, what are you doing?' asked the Grammar Wizard.

'Wrr... I gives him some sand.'

K slowly untied the string of the pouch.

The Grammar Wizard said, 'You have found *The Grammar of Spells*. Where could it have been? Of course. The book must have been in the Spelling Room all this time. You made anti-grammatical sand, yesterday, when there was a full moon.'

'You were always sooo clever.'

K was holding a pinch of sand in his gloved hand. He took three steps forward, and he sprinkled the sand onto the Grammar Wizard's wrist.

'Nooo!' she screamed.

She dropped the orange teacup she was holding. It shattered into nine pieces. The Grammar Wizard staggered towards the bookcase. She stretched her arms to touch the handle of the Lamp of Grammar. Before she could do so, she collapsed.

K stepped over the Grammar Wizard to reach the bookcase. His lips were quivering as he neared the lamp. He removed his gloves. He folded them and placed them in his pocket. K caressed the owlish eyes of the lamp.

M was in the kitchen and the door was half open. Peeking into the room, she saw the shattered pieces of the teacup that were on the floor.

The Grand Librarian stared at the fallen Grammar Wizard.

Woo, our Grammar Wizard is so sensitive to bad grammar that even a few grains of sand make her faint.'

'I does not care about... wrr... grammar.'

'When I become the Grammar Wizard, I shall make you the head of all the word-peckers. You would like that, wouldn't you?'

'Wrrr...Wrrr...'

Ha knocked at the door. K opened it, and he politely asked Ha to come in. After Ha entered the room, K threw some anti-grammatical sand on his neck.

'Is there anybody else in the cottage?' asked K.

'Yes… Wrr… M, the Grammar Wizard's assistant are here.'

'Where is she?'

'She are in… wrr… the kitchen.'

M noiselessly closed the door. She searched for a place to hide.

What should I do? Is the Grammar Wizard alright? How can I escape from here?

Looking through the window, she saw the mountains in the distance.

M said, 'Garden of Grammar, save me!'

K placed his pouch on the table. Holding a pinch of sand, he went to the kitchen door.

'M, my dear, are you here?'

M saw the flower that Q had plucked. It was in a blue vase on the table.

Closing her eyes, she whispered, 'If I were a grammatica flower, I would be so happy.'

K turned the doorknob and charged in. On the stove, beans were cooking in a pot of blue ink. A few carrots, chopped into circles, were on a cutting board. On the table, there was a black grammatica flower in a blue vase.

'Woo, there's no one here,' K said, with a scowl.

'Wrrr… That are strange. I seen her going into the kitchen.'

'Why is there a stupid grammatica flower on the floor? M must be in the cottage. She was here only moments ago. Woo search all the rooms.'

'I hates… wrr… grammatica flowers.'

CHAPTER 14

The Word Fields: Clauses I

Dots of starlight crisscrossed the choppy surface of the ink. It was past midnight. P and Q were on the shores of the Sea of Wishes. Q remembered being chased by a shark. Tonight, he was not going to be a goldfish.

'Can I make a wish again?' he asked.

'What kind of fish do you wish to be?'

Q swallowed his pill.

'If I were an elephant, I would cross this sea.'

'An elephant! Do elephants swim?' said P.

It was too late. He was standing next to a six-ton elephant. It flapped its large ears. Its tail swung from side to side, as it sauntered to the sea. It sucked ink into its trunk and squirted it out. Some salty ink fell on P. Trumpeting loudly, the elephant charged into the waves.

P swallowed his pill.

'If I were a seagull, I would cross this sea.'

The seagull took to the sky. It searched for the elephant, but all the bird could see was the

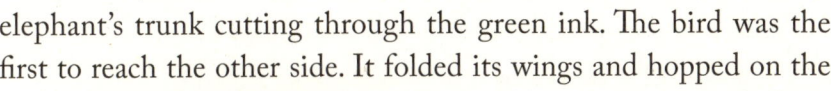

elephant's trunk cutting through the green ink. The bird was the first to reach the other side. It folded its wings and hopped on the sand. The elephant waded out of the ink, trampling on the tiny, shallow footprints of the seagull.

P and Q transformed into their original selves.

'This was much better than the last time,' said Q.

'Next time, I'll be an elephant. It looks like you had more fun.'

P opened the green door and they crossed into the First Conditional Zone. Pil was waiting for them. His bony hands clutched the handle of a walking stick.

'What happened?' asked P.

'My brother arrived from Biblios yesterday. The whole town is in panic. The spell-checker owls say that the Grammar Wizard has been kidnapped,' said Pil.

'Kidnapped! When did this happen?' asked P.

'Three days ago.'

'But we were away for just two days,' Q said.

Pil said, 'Time in the Second and Third Conditional Zones flows much slower than it does in the other parts of the Dimension. One day there is equal to two days everywhere else. Don't forget, they are the unreal zones.'

'Yes, we've actually been away for four days,' P said.

'There's a message from a bookworm named Wow,' said Pil. 'The message is: Word Fields.'

They walked in silence past the fields of corn and reached Pil's village.

'Thank you for looking after our balloon,' said P.

Pil nodded his head and removed his hat.

'I hope you find the Grammar Wizard soon.'

P and Q headed to the Word Fields. To get there faster, P turned the propellers on.

'How could anyone get past Ha?' Q asked.

'Mmm... Whoever kidnapped the Grammar Wizard must be someone who usually visits the Garden of Grammar.'

Their destination was far away. Q had time to go through his notes from the conditional zones. He could not believe that he had been a goldfish and an elephant.

'We have arrived,' said P.

The Word Fields were the largest flatlands in the Grammar Dimension. The fields were divided into twenty-one squares and one rectangular-shaped Sentence Assembly Area. Word-peckers made words, phrases, and clauses in the different squares. The spell-checker owls put everything together in the Sentence Assembly Area.

The balloon landed near the Sentence Assembly Area. Ha and Wow were waiting for them.

'What happened?' asked P.

Ha's left hand was clenched into a fist. In his other hand, he held a blue grammatica flower.

'It would be better if Wow tells you.'

The bookworm had wrapped itself around the stem of Ha's flower.

Wow said, 'The Grand Librarian K... He found *The Grammar of Spells* and made anti-grammatical sand. Woo, the word-pecker from the cottage, got him the sand from the Second Conditional Zone. I went to the cottage as soon as I could. I wanted to warn Ha. I was too late. When I arrived, he was lying on the floor. And there was no sign of K.'

Ha said, 'After I left K at the door of the cottage, I spoke with some flowers. They told me that the visitor had evil plans. I told them it was the Grand Librarian. They had nothing to worry about. The flowers insisted I go back to make sure the Grammar Wizard was safe. When I went to the cottage, K told me she had fainted. He asked me to come inside to help her. I went inside. I fainted. Later, Wow told me K had made anti-grammatical sand. I should have listened to those flowers. I completely missed their warning.'

'It was not your fault Ha,' said P. 'None of us expected the Grand Librarian to do such a thing.'

'After I recovered from the effects of the sand, I searched for K's boat. It was no longer there. He could have taken her anywhere by now,' said Ha.

'Bookworms are searching the entire Dimension for her. We will find her soon,' said Wow.

'What about M?' asked Q.

'I do not know where she is. I hope she escaped,' said Ha. 'I found a flower in the kitchen. It might be the one you plucked for your wife. You should have it.'

Ha gave the flower to Q. He gazed at the blue petals, wondering whether it was the flower he had plucked. He tucked the flower into his breast pocket.

'What do we do now?' asked Wow.

'When I was with the Grammar Wizard, she told me that whatever happens, Q must finish exploring the Dimension,' replied P.

'Then what are we waiting for? Q, this is the Word Fields,' said Wow. 'This is where sentences are made. Hmm… You do know what a sentence is, don't you?'

'Well, I really don't know how to define it.'

'The Grammar Council is still searching for a definition on what a sentence is. For the time being, I'll define a sentence as a group of words that has a subject and a predicate. A sentence expresses a complete thought.'

'And what's a predicate?'

'A predicate is a group of words that has a verb, and it gives information about the subject,' replied Wow.

'*I am in the Word Fields*. So, *I* is the subject, and "*am in the Word Fields*" is the predicate.'

'Exactly… Now, I'll talk about the object of a sentence. The object is something that receives an action from the subject.'

'Can you give me an example?'

'*I wrote a song*. Here, *I* is the subject, *wrote* is the verb, and *song* is the object,' Wow said.

'Also, "*wrote a song*" is the predicate of the sentence.'

'A sentence can also have an indirect object. Listen to this. *I wrote a song for the children.*'

'I'm guessing the noun *children* is the indirect object,' said Q.

'Yes, it is. The indirect object answers the question *for whom* or *to whom*. I wrote a song *for the children*.'

'Let me try. *I sent a flower to my wife.*'

'What is your direct object? What's your indirect object?'

'Well, *flower* is certainly the direct object of my action. *I sent a flower*. And when I ask the question *to whom*: it is to my wife. So, the indirect object should be *wife*.'

'Exactly... If you read the two sentences carefully, you'll notice a pattern. The direct object is usually a thing, and the indirect object is usually a person.'

Q wrote:

I wrote a song for the children.

I sent a flower to my wife.

'Mmm... I see what you mean. In these two sentences, the direct objects are *song* and *flower,* and the indirect objects are *children* and *wife.*'

'Exactly. Now, we are ready to talk about independent clauses. An independent clause has a subject and a predicate. It expresses a complete thought,' said Wow.

'*We are eating commas.* Is it an independent clause?'

'You tell me.'

'*We* is the subject and "*are eating commas*" is the predicate. And the clause makes sense by itself. It's an independent clause.'

'Exactly.'

'Well, independent clauses seem straightforward enough. I'm sure dependent clauses would be much more difficult to learn.'

'Don't worry. We are in the Word Fields. This is the best place to learn about dependent clauses,' said Wow. 'Now... A dependent clause has a subject and a predicate. However, it does not form a complete thought on its own. A dependent clause cannot stand on its own. It has to *lean* on an independent clause.'

'For example?'

'Well... Here's an example of a dependent clause: *while we were eating commas.*'

'Ahhh... That clause doesn't make sense on its own.'

'Exactly. Before we talk more about dependent clauses, I'll tell you about where we are in the Word Fields. Over there are squares for dependent clauses. We'll look at three types of *dependent clauses.*'

There's a square for *relative clauses*, another one for *adverbial clauses*, and another for *nominal clauses*. Those other squares are for making phrases. Pick me up,' said Wow.

They entered the Square of Relative Clauses. Q saw the word-peckers chipping away at pieces of wood. He listened to the sound of the word-peckers' beaks hitting the wood. The sound had a rhythm to it: peck, peckpeck; peck, peckpeck; peck, peckpeck.

'I'll define what a relative clause is. It identifies the person or thing in a sentence. And it gives us more information about this person or thing. A relative clause starts with a relative pronoun, of course,' said Wow.

Q frowned.

'But what's a relative pronoun?'

'Hmm… Weren't you at the Circle of Magic Trees? The tree representing pronouns should have told you.'

'Wait! I've a twig from that tree. The tree told me I would use it to find out about relative pronouns when the time is right. I guess the time is now.'

Q searched all seven of his pockets. The twig was in his upper-left inner coat pocket. Even after all these days, it still looked fresh.

'That tree is so wise. Now, cover the twig with some earth,' said Wow.

Using his hands, Q dug a hole. He placed the twig in it. He covered the hole with the rich black soil of the Word Fields.

'How long will it take to grow?' asked Q.

'Oh, I think something will happen sooner than you expect.'

At the spot where the twig was buried, a tree grew. It was not a big tree: it reached till Q's knees. The tree had three delicate branches on which rectangular-shaped leaves sprouted.

'Wait for a while. You'll be able to read the leaves,' said Wow.

'These leaves. They remind me of the magic trees' leaves.'

'They have the same shape, just a bit smaller.'

Words appeared on the leaves. They were—*who, which, whom, that,* and *whose.*

'So, here we have common relative pronouns,' said Wow.

Q stroked a leaf. It was a bit rough, like sandpaper.

'A relative pronoun introduces a relative clause. Give me an example,' said Wow.

'I spoke with a man *who is learning about relative clauses.*'

'Yes. The group of words, "*who is learning about relative clauses*", identifies and gives us more information about the noun *man.* Make a sentence using another relative pronoun.'

'This is the balloon *which I travelled in.*'

'Yes. The relative clause *"which I travelled in"* identifies and gives us more information about the noun *balloon*.'

'Here is a sentence with the relative pronoun *whom*. She was the woman *whom we met at the poetry festival.*'

'I haven't eaten a good poem this month. Your sentence is correct, by the way,' said Wow.

'How does this sound? She was the woman *who we met at the poetry festival.*'

'Well, these days, *whom* is seen as quite formal. We can replace the relative pronoun *whom* with the relative pronoun *who*.'

'So, what I said is correct.'

'Yes, it is. We can also leave out the relative pronoun in a sentence when the pronoun is the object of the clause.'

Q wrote the sentence: *She was the woman who we met at the poetry festival.*

'Mmm... So, here, the clause is: *who we met at the poetry festival.*'

'What is the subject of the clause?' asked Wow.

'It's *we*. And the object of the clause is *who*—referring to the woman.'

'Exactly! Since the relative pronoun, who, is the object of the clause, the pronoun can be left out.'

'*She was the woman we met at the poetry festival.* I like it.'

'Exactly.'

'How about this?'

Q scribbled a sentence: *She is the woman who recited a poem.*

'Is the relative pronoun the subject or the object in the clause?' asked Wow.

'Ahh. In my sentence, the relative pronoun, *who*, is the subject of the clause. So, we cannot leave it out.'

'Exactly. More sentences.'

'He is the student *that* won the debate.'

'Good... Now, "*that*" is an interesting relative pronoun. It can replace *who* or *which*.'

'So, it can be: He is the student *who* won the debate.'

'Yes.'

'And we can say: He is the student *which* won the debate.'

'No! We cannot use the relative pronoun *which* with a person.'

'I should've known that.'

In his notebook, Q read the sentence: This is the balloon *which* I travelled in.

In his mind, he replaced *which* with *that*.

'This is the balloon *that* I travelled in.'

'Very good. Now, make a sentence with the relative pronoun *whose*.'

'This is my friend *whose* home is in the shape of the letter Z.'

'Yes. Don't forget we also use the relative pronoun *whose* for things,' said Wow.

'I didn't know that.'

'Of course, we do. Listen to this: This is the quill pen *whose* owner is my friend.'

'Ahhh.'

'So... We use the relative pronouns *who* and *whom* only for people. We use the relative pronoun *which* for things and ideas. We use the relative pronoun *that* for things, ideas, and people. We use the relative pronoun *whose* for things and people,' said Wow.

Q wrote down everything he had learnt about relative clauses. He then sketched the tiny tree with its rectangular leaves.

Wow said, 'I used to come here when I was a young bookworm. I was friends with two spell-checker owls that were my age. We used to spend lots of time at the Square of Words.'

'What did you do there?'

'Oh. We just loved to hear word-peckers make words. Sometimes, we would even invent new words and ask the word-peckers to make them for us. They never listened to us!'

'Can you do that? Make new words?'

'Do you know the meaning of the word—wogret?'

Tapping his forehead with his index fingers, Q thought hard about the word.

'I haven't heard it before.'

'When you eat a word and wish you hadn't done so, that's when you have a wogret. Bookworms have a saying: Have no wogrets. Every word should be tasted.'

'Wow, did you just make the word up?'

'Before we leave this square, I'll tell you something important. All relative clauses are either defining or non-defining clauses. A defining clause identifies the person or thing in a sentence. And it is essential to the meaning of the sentence. *The lady who inaugurated the bookshop is calling us.* The clause "*who inaugurated the bookshop*" identifies the lady who is calling us.'

'I understand. If that clause were not there, we wouldn't know who is calling us.'

'Exactly.'

Q thought about the defining clause in the sentence.

'Do we put a comma before the clause: *who inaugurated the bookshop?*' he asked.

'When the clause is a defining clause, we do not use commas to mark it off from the rest of the sentence.'

'Can you give me an example of a non-defining clause?'

'First, I'll define what a non-defining clause is. A non-defining clause describes the person or thing in a sentence, but this clause is not essential to the message of the sentence. Write this down: The Grammar Wizard *comma* who I met at the new bookshop *comma* is calling us. What's the main message?'

Q wrote: *The Grammar Wizard, who I met at the new bookshop, is calling us.*

'The clause "*who I met at the new bookshop*" is an extra piece of information. We can still understand the essence of the sentence without this clause. The essence of the sentence is: The Grammar Wizard is calling us.'

'Exactly. A non-defining clause is ... well, non-defining. It is not essential to the meaning of a sentence. Non-defining clauses are marked off with commas.'

'One more example?' asked Q, twirling his pencil.

The bookworm removed its golden spectacles and gazed at the cloudless sky.

'*Words which are made in the Word Fields are important.* And then write the same sentence again. This time, use commas to separate the clause from the rest of the sentence.'

'Mmm,' mumbled Q, as he slowly placed the commas.

'How are the two sentences different in meaning?'

Q could not find any difference. He read the sentences backwards. He turned his notebook around, and the two sentences were upside down. Doing this did not help. He read the words again and again.

Words which are made in the Word Fields are important.

Words, which are made in the Word Fields, are important.

'Aha! I've got it. In the first sentence we are talking about those words which are made in the Word Fields. Those words are important. While in the second sentence, we are talking about words in general. All words are important. And there is an extra piece of information: words are made in the Word Fields.'

'Exactly!'

'Wow! Commas make such a difference.'

'We'll talk more about commas when we are in the Punctuation Grove. Here's another sentence. This house *comma* that is painted blue *comma* has sixteen windows.'

Q wrote: *This house, that is painted blue, has sixteen windows.*

'There is a non-defining clause: *that is painted blue.* The essence of the sentence is that the house has sixteen windows.'

'Focus on the non-defining clause.'

'Well, I would say it differently. This house, *which* is painted blue, has sixteen windows.'

'You're right. When we have a non-defining clause, we usually don't use the relative pronoun *that*. We use the relative pronoun *which* instead.'

'I drank some grammar potion in the Third Conditional Zone. It's really helping me understand clauses.'

'Mmm… Maybe… Well… Okay… Go to another square.'

A spell-checker owl was on a treetop. It spotted the shape of a bookworm on Q's shoulder. The owl glided down and landed on a long relative clause.

The owl said, 'Excuse me. Are you Wow from the Grand Library?'

'Yes.'

'You are a true grammatical creature. I have a question for you. Do you notice anything unusual in this square?'

'Not really. Why?'

'Someone has stolen some relative clauses. The word-peckers are afraid to work here. We may have a shortage of relative clauses soon,' the owl said.

Q said, 'I remember the Grammar Wizard told us about this. Maybe, it's all K's doing.'

The owl's ears twitched. It spread its wings and flew away.

CHAPTER 15

The Word Fields: Clauses II

Q entered the next square by hopping over a line of familiar looking flowers.

'Are these grammatica flowers?' he asked.

'Yes, they mark the boundaries of the different sections of the Word Fields.'

At the Square of Adverbial Clauses, a word-pecker stopped pecking. Bending its neck back, it shook its body.

'What's an adverb?' Wow asked.

'Ah, adverbs… Adverbs are words which modify verbs, adjectives, and other adverbs,' replied Q.

'Good. Adverbs answer questions such as *when, where, how, why,* and *to what extent.* An adverbial clause is a dependent clause that acts like an adverb in a sentence. And so, an adverbial clause modifies a verb, an adjective, or an adverb. An adverbial clause starts with a subordinating conjunction. I'll talk about four groups of adverbial clauses.'

Q remembered that a magic tree told him something about subordinating conjunctions. He flipped through the pages of his notebook, and he found three subordinating conjunctions: *because, although,* and *when.* Q was thinking about the tree representing conjunctions with its long, thin branches. The tree was angry when...

'Stop daydreaming! In the first group, there are adverbial clauses of time. They start with subordinating conjunctions such as *after, before*, and *when*,' said Wow.

'Umm... I will meet you *after I finish listening to the ghost story*.'

'Yes. In the second group, there are adverbial clauses of reason. Could you tell me what subordinating conjunctions we use with this group of adverbial clauses?'

'*Since we are in the Word Fields*, I can see how sentences are made.'

'Very good. We use subordinating conjunctions such as *since* and *because* in adverbial clauses of reason.'

'I don't know much about clauses *because I never paid much attention to my grammar*.'

'Better late than never... The third group is about adverbial clauses of contrast. We use subordinating conjunctions such as *although, despite*, and *however*.'

'*Although I have learnt a lot*, I'm still not tired.'

'Glad to hear it. For the fourth group... These are adverbial clauses of condition that have subordinating conjunctions such as *if* and *unless*.'

'*Unless we stop the Grand Librarian*, all will be lost.'

'I'm afraid you're right.'

Q made notes on the four adverbial clauses.

Wow asked, 'May I walk on your page?'

Q placed the bookworm below his sentence. It marched from left to right.

'You are missing something here. In a sentence where the adverbial clause comes before the independent clause, you should place a comma to separate the two clauses. Look at what you have written,' Wow said.

Unless we stop the Grand Librarian all will be lost.

Q read the sentence carefully.

'There has to be a comma after *Librarian*,' said Wow.

Q added the comma.

Unless we stop the Grand Librarian, all will be lost.

He glanced around and spotted a group of trees.

'Could we spend some time in the shade?' asked Q.

They went to a large tree that was covered in oval-shaped leaves. Wow climbed onto a large leaf. It quivered as the bookworm restlessly shuffled back and forth.

'Q, something just isn't right. Word-peckers absolutely love making adverbial clauses. When they are here, they sing songs and make fun of each other. They usually make a lot of noise. Word-peckers from other squares come here to relax. There's a pond of black ink nearby. This was always the liveliest square in the Word Fields. Today, it's so quiet. I've never seen it like this before.'

They rested for a few minutes, before going to the next square.

The sign said: Square of Nominal Clauses.

'Oh. What do they do?' asked Q.

'A nominal clause is a dependent clause that acts like a noun or a pronoun in a sentence. Look at the clauses on the ground.'

that he is listening

whatever you write

what I am looking for

'Can you make sentences using these nominal clauses?' asked Wow.

Q wrote:

That he is listening is good news.

Whatever you write must come from your heart.

I have found *what I am looking for.*

'You may become a writer one day,' said Wow. 'In your first two sentences, the nominal clause is the subject in the sentence.'

'Yes. And in the last sentence, the nominal clause is the object of the sentence.'

'A nominal clause functions like a noun. In a sentence, it can take any place a noun takes. Well then, that's all you need to know about clauses. Walk that-a-way.'

A flock of word-peckers flew quietly above them. Some birds were flying slower than others. The birds were not flying in a proper W formation. It seemed to Q that the birds formed an irregular V.

CHAPTER 16

The Word Fields: Phrases

'A phrase is a group of words that forms a part of a clause or a sentence. Now, there are many different types of phrases. I'll talk about five of them: noun phrases, verb phrases, adjectival phrases, adverbial phrases, and prepositional phrases. I'll start with some noun phrases,' said Wow.

On the grass, two word-peckers were dipping their beaks in a basin of black ink.

'Why are they doing that?' asked Q, walking towards the birds.

'Oh, they're resting. The black ink cools their beaks.'

One of the word-peckers saw the visitors.

The bird asked, 'Wrr... Will Woo be in-charge of the Word Fields? Really? Wrr... Really? Really?'

'How could you say such a thing?' asked Wow.

'It's what my friends are saying. Wrr... Woo will be our boss, wrrr... our boss,' replied the bird.

'Woo cannot even make a grammatically correct sentence,' said Wow, 'How can that bird be your boss?'

The word-peckers stared blankly at the horizon. Ink dribbled from their beaks and onto their necks. The birds were lost in thought. They even forgot to dip their beaks into the black ink.

'Go to those phrases,' whispered Wow.

Q said, 'I'm sure K knows all the rules of grammar, very, very well. How can I ever defeat him in a grammar contest?'

'Grammar is not only about rules. It's much more than that. It's about how you feel about words, language, and people. And we don't know what he is planning to do. Now is not the time to think of such things. Let's learn all we can from the Word Fields.'

'Mmm... You're right. I guess.'

They passed a signboard: Square of Noun Phrases.

'A noun phrase is a group of words in which the most important word is a noun or a pronoun. A noun phrase can also just be a noun or pronoun. A noun phrase acts like a noun in a sentence,' said Wow.

Q read the noun phrases which were near his feet.

notebook

two spell-checker owls

a lot of patience

'In these phrases the nouns are the most important words. For example, in the second phrase, the most important word is: *owls*,' said Wow.

'And the other words in the phrase—*two and spell-checker*—modify the noun *owls*.'

'Exactly... Make sentences using these noun phrases.'

Q wrote down:

I go everywhere with my *notebook.*

Two spell-checker owls are on the Grammar Council.

It takes *a lot of patience* to teach grammar.

'I completely agree with your last sentence,' said Wow.

'I don't think I'll ever be able to teach grammar.'

They went to the next square. In this square, verb phrases were scattered all over the ground.

'A verb phrase is a verb plus an auxiliary verb,' said Wow.

'What are auxiliary verbs?'

'They are verbs that help the main verbs. Read these two phrases. I'm sure you can tell me what the auxiliary verbs are.'

The two verb phrases were:

has written

am spelling

'Mmm... So, *has* is the auxiliary verb for the verb *written*,' said Q.

'Yes, it is. For the phrase—*am spelling*...'

'And *am* is the auxiliary verb for the verb *spelling*.'

'Yes,' said Wow. 'Make sentences.'

Q wrote down these sentences:

She *has written* in her diary.

I *am spelling* her name.

'Good. Now, jump over that stream of black ink.'

They entered the Square of Adjectival Phrases.

Q read the phrases:

smart, young

cool and starry

long, blue

'Well, what do you think?' asked Wow.

'In these phrases, the adjectives are the most important words. Let me see if I can use the first phrase in a sentence. A *smart, young man* is walking in the Word Fields.'

'More sentences.'

'It was a *cool and starry* evening. My wife was wearing a *long, blue* dress.'

'Any questions?'

'Not really... Just to be clear, an adjectival phrase is a group of words which acts as an adjective in a sentence. So, in my sentence, the phrase '*cool and starry*' acts as an adjective to the noun *evening*.'

'It's as simple as that.'

A spell-checker owl glided above them as they walked to the next square, the Square of Adverbial Phrases.

'Wow... An owl is following us. Its shadow has been near us ever since we entered the Square of Noun Phrases,' whispered Q.

'The owl might be working for K. Let's pretend we haven't seen it.'

'You've known K for a long time. Did you ever think he could make anti-grammatical sand?'

'The K I knew was dedicated to the Grand Library. He took such good care of the books. He fed the goldfish every day, organised so many events for our library members, and wanted everyone to read as many books as possible. I've seen him arranging books till midnight. Every Monday, he would select the best books for me to eat words from. I thought he would always be the Grand Librarian. I never imagined anything would change.'

They came to three adverbial phrases. Q read them out:

by the river

three times a day

very carefully

'An adverbial phrase is a group of words that acts as an adverb in a sentence. An adverbial phrase modifies a verb, an adjective, and an adverb. Make some sentences with these phrases,' said Wow.

'I'll have to think about this.'

'Take your time.'

Curling up into a circle, the bookworm took a nap. Wow dreamt of semicolons and colons, but mostly of semicolons.

Q sat down under a tree, resting his back on its trunk. He wrote:

She is reading *by the river*.

Wow takes a nap *three times a day*.

Word-peckers make words *very carefully*.

'I've finished,' said Q.

The bookworm woke up, and it stretched all its left legs. It yawned, twice. It then read the second sentence.

'Are you making fun of me?'

'These are the only sentences I could think of.'

The bookworm dashed down Q's arm. After it reached the end of his fingers, it turned around. It quickly marched ahead, and it halted on his open palm. It twisted its body into the shape of the letter *e*. Twisting some more, it took the shape of the letter *s*.

'Wow, what are you doing?'

'I get excited just thinking about prepositional phrases.'

'Why?'

'I love going under, between, and over things.'

Unlike in the other squares, where the phrases were on the ground, the phrases in this square were all over the place. A phrase was dangling from the branch of a tree. Another phrase was in a stream of black ink. And one was half-buried in the ground. Q had to search for phrases.

The ones he found were:

with the thesaurus

from the Word Fields

between you and me

Wow said, 'A prepositional phrase is made up of a preposition and a noun phrase. Prepositional phrases have many functions. We won't have time to talk about all of them. I'll tell you about three functions. The first, modifying verbs, nouns, and adjectives. See these fabulous phrases around you.'

'She is talking to the boy *with the thesaurus*.'

'Good, good… The prepositional phrase, *with the thesaurus*, modifies the noun *boy*.'

'The second function: acting like an adverbial phrase of time or place.'

'I enjoy reading sentences *from the Word Fields*.'

'Yes. Your prepositional phrase acts as an adverbial phrase of place.'

'The third function: modifying a clause.'

'*Between you and me*, I wish we'll find the Grammar Wizard soon.'

'In what you just said, the prepositional phrase is modifying a clause,' said Wow.

The bookworm clutched Q's earlobe and whispered, 'Many people don't know why we say *between you and me*, and not *between you and I*. Do you know why?'

'No.'

'The noun or pronoun in a prepositional phrase is called the object of the preposition. And the pronoun takes the objective case. Do you remember what the objective cases of the pronouns *I* and *you* are?'

'Well... The objective case for *I* is *me* and for *you* is *you*.'

'Exactly. And so, we say*: between you and me.*'

'Between you and me, I believe K could make Woo the head of the Word Fields,' said Q.

'Between you and me, if that happens, it will spell disaster for us all.'

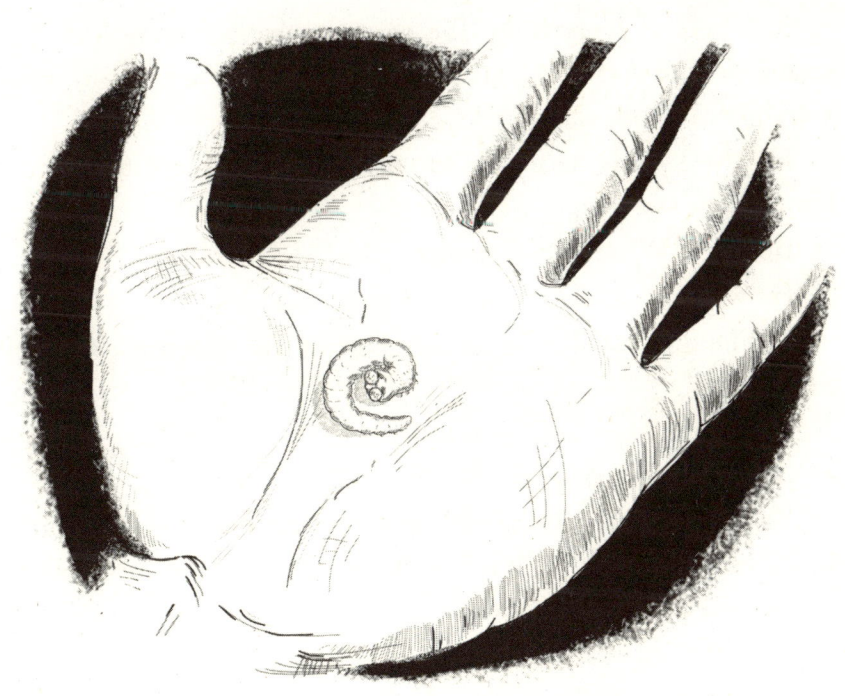

CHAPTER 17

The Word Fields: Sentences

P and Ha walked towards the balloon. P's hands were clasped behind his back.

'K is behind everything. The negative abstract noun leak. The attack on the Articles Station. All those rumours about anti-grammatical sand,' said P.

'He thinks it is necessary to create confusion and fear in the Dimension,' said Ha.

'But why? What does K want?'

'He wants to change the rules of grammar.'

'It'll be difficult. The other members on the Grammar Council won't agree.'

'He can threaten them with anti-grammatical sand. They will have no choice but to agree,' said Ha.

'Yes, it's possible. But the spell-checker owls will never accept him as the new Grammar Wizard. Without their support, he won't be able to make any real changes.'

They stopped talking when they saw Q.

'Any news about the Grammar Wizard?' asked Wow.

'Not yet. We still feel it would be best for Q to visit the Punctuation Grove,' said P.

'The grove isn't far away. Could we spend some more time here? He really should know about the four types of sentence structures,' said Wow.

'Come back soon,' said P.

Q and Wow were at the Sentence Assembly Area.

'Do you remember what the definition of a sentence is?' asked Wow.

'It has a subject and a predicate. And it expresses a complete thought.'

'Exactly. Now, let's see how sentences are made in the Word Fields. Spell-checker owls collect words, phrases, clauses, and punctuation marks, and join them to form sentences.'

'What happens when they finish making a sentence?'

'You see those frames over there? Once a sentence is made, it is put into a frame. Framed sentences from the Word Fields are appreciated all over the Dimension. People discuss these sentences. Sometimes, they give ideas to writers, poets, and even painters. They're especially popular in Writers' Block.'

There was a golden frame leaning on a tree. It looked like the frame one uses to frame a painting.

'Oh yes. I saw one in Biblios. The words were: *Grammar is in the details*. Now that I think about it, there are a few in Alphabet Village as well. I never took the time to read them,' said Q.

'Look, an owl has just formed a sentence.'

The sentence in the grass was: *I read two stories.*

'It's a simple sentence. A simple sentence has one clause. And it expresses a complete thought. So, it can stand on its own,' said Wow.

'Sounds like an independent clause to me.'

'It is an independent clause.'

'So, a simple sentence is an independent clause. That's interesting.'

'Yes, it is. Write this down. *Yesterday, I read aloud two short stories to three young spell-checker owls.* What type of sentence is it?'

'Well… *Yesterday* is an adverb; *aloud* is another adverb; *two* is an adjective; *short* is an adjective; *stories* is the object of the sentence; and *"to three young spell-checker owls"* is a prepositional phrase. The subject is *I*. The verb is *read*. So, there is a subject and a verb. And the sentence expresses a complete thought. It's a simple sentence. Am I right?'

'Exactly. I just added some modifiers to the initial sentence. It is still a simple sentence.'

'What's the next type of sentence?'

'A compound sentence.'

The bookworm pressed its glasses closer to its eyes and surveyed the field. Two spell-checker owls were placing two groups of words next to each other. The owls flew to a nearby branch. They gazed at their newly created sentence.

'And what are they doing?' asked Q.

'My guess is those two owls have joined two independent clauses.'

'What type of sentence has two independent clauses?'

'When you have two independent clauses in one sentence, it's a compound sentence. In a compound sentence, both the clauses have equal grammatical importance.'

Q walked to the sentence, stopping before its full stop. He made sure he was not blocking the view of the two owls.

The sentence was: *I have read a thousand books in the Grand Library, but I still have a lot more to learn.*

'My guess was right. It's a compound sentence! Can you identify the independent clauses?' said Wow.

'There are two independent clauses—*I have read a thousand books in the Grand Library*, and *I still have a lot more to learn.*'

'Exactly.'

'Does every compound sentence have the word *but*?'

'Oh no… We can use other words as well. These words are called co-ordinating conjunctions. A common co-ordinating conjunction is *and*. Other co-ordinating conjunctions are—*or, so, yet*.'

'I use compound sentences all the time, and I don't even know it,' said Q.

The bookworm said, 'Put me down on a blank page of your notebook. Pour some ink in the middle of the page.'

Q found a pool of black ink. Cupping his hands, he scooped up some ink. He poured the ink onto the page. Standing near the puddle of ink, the bookworm dipped all twenty-six left legs into the puddle. It wrote words by moving its left legs. Sometimes, it would write with six or seven left legs, keeping the other left legs up in the air. It was writing many letters at the same time. When it wanted to move ahead, it put all its weight on its right legs (which were dry) and hopped forward. Then, the bookworm put its left legs down and wrote some more. When it needed more ink, it hopped back to the puddle. All of this was done in a jiffy.

'You have beautiful handwriting, I mean… eh… leg-writing,' said Q.

'Thank you. Read what I have written.'

I have read a thousand books in the Grand Library; I still have a lot more to learn.

'There's a semicolon. How come?' said Q.

'In my compound sentence, the two independent clauses are joined by a semicolon. We'll talk more about semicolons in the Punctuation Grove.'

Q made some notes on compound sentences.

'So, we join two independent clauses with a co-ordinating conjunction or with a semicolon.'

'Exactly. Don't forget, in a compound sentence the two independent clauses should be closely related to each other.'

The two spell-checker owls were still in the tree. Their eyes were glued to the compound sentence. One owl cocked its head to the right and then to the left. The other owl was hanging upside down.

Q asked, 'What are these owls thinking so hard about? How long does it take to make a sentence?'

'Ooh… They could take days to decide whether they like it or not. You see… They focus on each word. They make sure they have chosen the right word. They see how each word relates to the other words. They talk about the use of punctuation. They imagine how the reader would feel after reading the sentence.'

'No wonder they take so much time.'

'I've even heard of spell-checker owls taking months to decide on a sentence. It is for this reason framed sentences from the Word Fields are so valuable,' said Wow. 'Now, tell me whether there is a dependent clause here.'

Q read a sentence that was near his feet.

I love drinking green ink that is from the Garden of Grammar.

'Mmm... There's a dependent clause in it. It is—*that is from the Garden of Grammar.*'

'And what type of dependent clause is it?'

'It's a relative clause. It gives us more information about the noun *ink.*'

'Exactly! A complex sentence has an independent clause and at least one dependent clause. The independent clause is grammatically more important than the dependent clause.'

'So *I love drinking green ink that is from the Garden of Grammar* is a complex sentence. It has an independent clause. *I love drinking green ink.* And it has a dependent clause: *that is from the Garden of Grammar,*' said Q.

'Exactly.'

'Mmm... I can see that the independent clause is grammatically more important than the dependent clause. The independent clause—*I love drinking green ink*—can stand on its own while the dependent clause—*that is from the Garden of Grammar*—cannot.'

'That's right. And how does it compare with a compound sentence?' asked Wow.

'In a compound sentence, both the clauses have equal grammatical importance.'

'Exactly.'

They found another complex sentence in the grass. Leaves covered many of its letters.

Bending down, Q blew the leaves away. He saw this:

He learned how to cook after he got married.

'What can you tell me about these clauses?' asked Wow.

'*He learned how to cook*. It's an independent clause. This clause can stand on its own. The dependent clause is: *after he got married*. The clause answers the question *when*. So, this should be an adverbial clause. Yes, I'm sure it is.'

'Exactly! Don't forget. When the adverbial clause comes first in a sentence…'

'It has to be followed by a comma.'

'Q, soon you'll be giving grammar lessons. Let's find a complex sentence with two dependent clauses. Ah, here is one.'

Although I came home late, I managed to make a dish which was quite tasty.

'Can you identify the clauses?' asked Wow.

'*Although I came home late*… It's an adverbial clause. I'm sure of it.'

'Go on.'

'The clause "*which was quite tasty*" says something about the noun *dish*, so the clause must be a relative clause.'

'Exactly. There are two dependent clauses in this complex sentence: the first one is an adverbial clause and the second one is a relative clause.'

'Are we done? I think it's time to go.'

Q could see P and Ha checking the propellers of the basket.

Wow said, 'I should show you the last type of sentence: a compound-complex sentence.'

'Brrr... Sounds like double trouble.'

'After all you've learnt, you'll have no trouble at all. A compound-complex sentence has at least two independent clauses and at least one dependent clause. There must be one somewhere close by.'

They searched for a compound-complex sentence. They found every type of sentence except that one.

Q mumbled, 'Compound-complex sentences... compound-complex sentences... compound-complex sentences.'

A spell-checker owl's ears are not parallel to each other. This helps it to hear faraway sounds.

An owl was gliding above the clouds over the Sentence Assembly Area. It heard Q say the words: compound-complex sentences. It spiralled down and circled Q's head.

'Are you looking for a compound-complex sentence?' asked the owl.

Wow looked up.

'Do you know where we can find one?'

'We haven't made that type of sentence for quite some time. Wait here. I'll assemble one just for you.'

The owl returned carrying three clauses—one held by its beak and two by its feet. It placed the clauses in the correct order. Without saying a word, the owl flapped its wings and disappeared into the thin, blue clouds.

'I recognise the owl. It was the same one that asked us about the missing relative clauses,' said Q.

'Read the sentence.'

The Grand Librarian has agreed to our demand, and he is going to ask Q thirteen questions which have been prepared by a committee of owls.

'It's a compound-complex sentence. Right?' said Q. 'The first two clauses are independent clauses, and the last one is a dependent clause.'

'Read it again. You haven't got the message.'

Q dropped to his knees. His trembling fingers ran over two words: *thirteen questions.*

Wow said in a quivering voice, 'Let's go… We must tell P and Ha about this compound-complex sentence.'

CHAPTER 18

Above the Word Fields: Subject–Verb Agreement

'The Grand Librarian has agreed to our demand, and he is going to ask Q thirteen questions which have been prepared by a committee of owls,' said Ha.

'Exactly. That was the message,' said Wow.

'Your owl has given us valuable information. The sentence tells us K cannot take over the Garden of Grammar as he planned to. The spell-checker owls have made it clear they will not accept it. It is good news,' said Ha.

'What do we do?' asked Q.

'All we can do is to go to the Punctuation Grove. K will contact us, somehow. After all, he needs to tell you where to meet him,' P replied.

Q wished that all of this was a bad dream, and that he would be waking up soon. He pinched himself hard. In just a few days, he had visited so many places in the Dimension. He had learnt so much grammar. He needed time to absorb everything.

'Well, he knows about the four types of sentences. I need to talk to him about subject-verb agreement,' said Wow.

'You can do it when we are in the sky,' said P.

They flew east towards the Punctuation Grove. Q crouched in a corner of the basket. His hands were locked around his knees. Wow marched around in a circle.

Ha and P were leaning on the side of the basket, and they were gazing at the black clouds.

'My guess is K took her to the Grand Library. There are so many rooms where he could keep her. To get to Biblios, he would not take the River of Green Ink. He could be easily seen. Instead, he would have sailed on the ocean, and gone around the Dimension to reach Biblios,' said Ha.

'I don't think so. K wouldn't dare take the Grammar Wizard out into the ocean. It's just too risky. If the boat gets caught in a strong current, he'll end up far away from land,' said P.

'Then where could he have taken her?' asked Ha.

'If I were K, I'd take her to the Third Conditional Zone. There are lots of unexplored areas there. I'm certain he's been there many times. Since bookworms fall ill in that zone, our bookworms won't be spending much time there.'

'Well, wherever she may be, we need to find her soon. When we were in the Word Fields, I saw that the word-peckers were not making as many words as they used to. What happens when they stop making words?'

They exchanged worried glances.

Wow said, 'Q! Time for some grammar… Let's talk about subject-verb agreement. I read five newspapers a day. I often find at least one sentence where the subject and the verb do not agree.'

'And what do you mean by *agree*?'

'It's quite simple, actually. When the subject is singular, the verb should be singular. When the subject is plural, the verb should be plural.'

'That sounds reasonable.'

'People still make mistakes. I'll start with collective nouns. Do you know what they are?'

'I do... A collective noun refers to a group of people, animals, or things that is taken as a singular noun.'

'Yes, examples of collective nouns are *audience, council*, and *team*,' said Wow. 'Now, if we see the collective noun as a unit, we use the singular verb.'

'The audience *was* watching the play.'

'In your sentence, we are not focusing on the individuals in the audience. We see the *audience* as a unit, and so we use the singular verb.'

'Yes, we see the audience as a group,' said P.

'And if we see the collective noun as a collection of individuals, we use a plural verb.'

'The audience *were* throwing flowers at the actors.'

'That's right. Make two more sentences with collective nouns.'

'Mmm... Before I do, answer this question: When was the Grammar Council established?'

'In the Year of the Full Stop,' said Wow.

'The Grammar Council *was* established in the Year of the Full Stop.'

'Yes. We use the singular verb *was* with the *Grammar Council*.'

'The Grammar Council *have* to agree on when to hold the spelling bee competition.'

'Excellent! Here, you're looking at the council as a collection of individuals. That's why you use the plural verb *have*.'

Q wrote down when to use a singular verb and when to use a plural verb.

'Now, I'll talk about prepositional phrases... Errors can happen when the noun in a prepositional phrase is taken as the subject of a sentence. Write this down: *The green ink in the cups are cool,*' Wow said.

Q focused on the group of words: *the cups are cool.* He read the sentence as a whole: The green ink in the cups are cool.

'It's correct. The noun *cups* is plural and it agrees with the verb *are,*' said Q.

'What is the subject?'

Q identified the different parts of the sentence. He realised that *'in the cups'* was a prepositional phrase. The subject of the sentence was: *ink.*

'The green ink in the cups *is* cool.'

'Exactly. Don't worry if you get it wrong the first time. Prepositional phrases in sentences confuse even me sometimes.'

'Woo, the word-pecker in the cottage… There was something wrong with all its sentences. And now I understand why. In all Woo's sentences, the subject and the verb never agree!'

'Yes. Those sentences sound so out of tune. Did you know that the Grammar Wizard invited Woo to stay with her? She wanted to help the word-pecker improve its grammar.'

'And now Woo is working against her.'

'It's hard to imagine that a word-pecker could be so unhappy in the Garden of Grammar, of all places.'

'I wonder why Woo's subject and verb never agree.'

'Once all of this is over, you can find out. I want to talk about another area where people make errors. Indefinite pronouns… Tell me a few indefinite pronouns.'

'*Anyone, somebody, everyone…*'

'Those are all singular indefinite pronouns. Is this correct? *Everyone are coming to the puppet show.*'

'I'm not sure… Doesn't *everyone* mean a lot of people? So, it should be correct.'

'No. Everyone means every person. We are talking about each person coming to the puppet show. It should be: *Everyone is...*,' said Wow.

Q wrote down:

Everyone is coming to the puppet show.

'Exactly... *Everyone, anyone, somebody.* They are all pronouns that take the singular form of the verb,' said Wow.

'Is *anyone* listening to me?'

'Good question... There are plural indefinite pronouns that take the plural form, such as *many* and *both*.'

'There are hundreds of word-peckers. *Many* have visited the Punctuation Grove.'

'Some plural indefinite pronouns, such as *all* and *some*, may or may not take a plural verb,' said Wow.

'And I can't believe I said subject-verb agreement is reasonable.'

'Where is the ink? *All* of it is gone.'

'Umm... The indefinite pronoun *all* stands for the subject *ink* which is an uncountable noun. And so, we use *is*.'

'Exactly. How about this? The bookshelf is full of bookworms. *All* are having brunch,' said Wow.

'The indefinite pronoun *all* stands for *bookworms*. The word *bookworms* is a plural noun. So, we say *are*,' said Q.

'You are speaking like a grammatical creature.'

'It must be the effects of the grammar potion.'

'Well... I suppose so.'

'I was wondering about something. What happens when we use *either...or*?' asked Q.

He wrote: *Either the word-pecker or the spell-checker owl is carrying the postcard.*

'It's correct. Here, only one bird is carrying the postcard. So, we use a singular verb,' said Wow.

'Makes sense to me. I hope we've finished talking about subject-verb agreement. I need a break.'

'We'll take one soon. Tell me whether this is correct. *Either the spell-checker owl or the word-peckers are in the field.*'

'I'm not sure,' said Q, biting into his pencil.

He tasted something sweet. He bit his pencil again. It tasted like cinnamon.

'When we have "*either...or*" or "*neither...nor*", the verb should agree with the noun closest to it,' said Wow.

'Since *word-peckers* are plural, we say—*are* in the field. The sentence is correct.'

'You are right. How about this? *Neither the word-peckers nor the spell-checker owl is in the field.*'

'It has to be correct,' said Q. 'The verb *is* agrees with the noun closest to it: *spell-checker owl*.'

'Exactly.'

'Can we take a break now?'

'Not yet. What about this? *The Grammar Wizard, along with the other members of the Grammar Council, are visiting the Punctuation Grove.*'

'It must be correct. After all, apart from the Grammar Wizard, there are six members on the Grammar Council, and so the verb should be plural.'

'It's incorrect. In my sentence, the subject is the Grammar Wizard. The phrase—*along with the other members of the Grammar Council*—is additional information,' said Wow.

'The Grammar Wizard, along with the other members of the Grammar Council, *is* visiting the Punctuation Grove.'

'Now, it's correct. To introduce additional information, we can say: *along with*, *in addition to*, or *as well as*. We mark off the additional information with commas.'

'Break?'

'After I tell you about two expressions, you can take your break,' said Wow. 'Listen very carefully… A number of bookworms *are* searching the Dimension for the Grammar Wizard. The number of words being made *is* going down.'

'Mmm… So, with "*a number*" we use the plural verb. And with "*the number*" we use the singular verb.'

'This should be enough for now. Don't forget in a sentence, the subject and the verb must agree with each other—always.'

Wow crawled into the folds of a blanket and was soon dreaming of dashes and hyphens.

Q joined P and Ha.

'How much longer till we reach the Punctuation Grove?' asked Q.

P replied, 'In half an hour or so.'

'I've been learning so much grammar over these past few days. I'm not sure I can remember everything,' said Q.

Ha said, 'The more you think about how grammar is used, the more naturally it will come to you. After some time, you would not have to think so much about it. You will become a grammatical creature'.

Q peered down to see where they were. A group of red clouds floated over the River of Black Ink. He found the shapes of the clouds to be familiar. The clouds were thin: some were curved, while others were straight lines.

'Are those letters?'

Ha and P exclaimed together: 'Word clouds!'

CHAPTER 19

The Punctuation Grove I

The word clouds faced the ground. Since Q was above the clouds, the shapes of the letters looked reversed to him. They were like the reflection of words in a mirror.

P positioned the propellers upwards: the balloon went below the word clouds. The message was:

Q
Come
alone to
the Garden
of Grammar.
I have some
questions for you.
K

'At last! We know where the Grammar Wizard is. She must have been in the Garden of Grammar all this time,' said Ha.

'The information the owl gave us is correct. K has thirteen questions for our Q,' said P.

They landed in the Punctuation Grove. The tangy smell of punctuation filled the balloon's basket.

'Wow, make sure you return when the spell-checker owls start hooting,' said P.

Q gazed at an apostrophe tree in wonder. Its black trunk was smooth and thin. All the branches were at the top. A bunch of apostrophes hung from the tip of each branch.

'We'll look at apostrophes later. I'll show you where the commas grow,' said Wow.

Arriving at the edge of a line of apostrophe trees, Q saw curved pieces of thick, black wire jutting out of the pink ground.

'This is the best soil for growing commas,' said Wow. 'Do you see them?'

'Ooh… So, that's what they are.'

What looked like curved pieces of wire to Q were the tails of commas.

'Lower me down to a comma,' said Wow.

The bookworm sniffed at the tail of a comma and nibbled at it.

'Yummy! It's ripe.'

'How is it taken out of the ground?'

'Hold its tail. First push it gently away from you. Then pull it towards you. Do you want to try?'

'Not really.'

'The first time may be a bit difficult.'

Q clutched the tail of a comma and pulled jerkily. The tail snapped.

'When dealing with punctuation, you need to take your time. Push and then pull. Don't be in a hurry,' said Wow.

Q grasped the tail of another comma. After taking a deep breath, he eased the comma from the soil.

'Congratulations!' said Wow.

'How come it's so big?'

'It has to be washed and kept in the sun for three days. It'll shrink in size.'

Q found a stream of black ink to soak the comma in. He left it on the ground to dry.

'What are commas used for?' he asked.

'Why don't you tell me?'

'Well, I know commas are used in lists.'

'Show me.'

Q opened his notebook to a blank yellow page. He wrote:

Please bring two pencils, some paperclips, a grammatica flower and a handful of commas.

'How many commas did you use?' asked Wow.

'Two.'

'What happens if you add another comma after the word *flower*? Will it change the meaning of the sentence?'

Q added a comma.

Please bring two pencils, some paperclips, a grammatica flower, and a handful of commas.

'Well, without a comma after *grammatica flower*, I could think that the two items, *a grammatica flower* and *a handful of commas*, are together as a unit. When I add a comma after *grammatica flower*, I'm sure that the two items, *a grammatica flower* and *a handful of commas*, are not to be taken as a unit,' Q replied.

'Correct. The last comma in the list has a name. It's called an Oxford comma. Some people use a comma with every item on the list while some others don't use a comma before the last item. They feel that the meaning of the sentence is clear without adding the last comma. They don't see the need to use the Oxford comma.'

'I'm a bit confused. Should I use the Oxford comma or not?'

'Well, if you feel that the meaning would be clearer by using an Oxford comma, go ahead and use it. However, if you feel that there is no need for the comma, then don't use it.'

'I'm still confused.'

'Okay. Write. *I am meeting my friends comma K and Woo full stop.*'

Q wrote—*I am meeting my friends, K and Woo.*

He read the sentence slowly, frowning as he got to the end.

'It looks like my friends are K and Woo. They are most definitely not.'

'Exactly... Now, add a comma after K.'

Q added the comma.

I am meeting my friends, K, and Woo.

'Much clearer! I'm meeting my friends, and I'm also meeting K and Woo,' said Q.

'There are times when it's a good idea to use an Oxford comma, just so that everything is crystal clear for the reader.'

'I agree.'

'Place me on the notebook. I need ink.'

Q poured some ink onto the middle of a page.

Wow dipped his left legs in the ink and wrote:

The actor, who is walking in the garden, is practising his lines.

Wow asked, 'Do you remember what a non-defining clause is?'

'A non-defining clause describes the subject. It's not the essential part of a sentence. In your sentence, the relative clause, *who is walking in the garden*, is a non-defining clause.'

'Exactly. When we have a non-defining clause, we mark it off with commas. Is there any other way to use a comma?'

The bookworm wrote a sentence. *Since I read many books, I know a lot about punctuation.*

'This looks familiar. It's a complex sentence. The first part of the sentence is an adverbial clause. When the adverbial clause comes before the independent clause, one should use a comma to separate the two clauses,' said Q.

'Exactly! Now, tell me whether this is correct or not.'

Wow's legs wrote—*I borrow books from the Grand Library, I read them by the Ocean of Ink.*

Q scratched the bridge of his nose.

'Mmm… I'm not sure.'

'It is grammatically incorrect. We should not use a comma to separate two independent clauses.'

'Couldn't we use a full stop instead of a comma?'

Wow shuffled to the tail of the comma which was still wet. He drank the ink. Slurp, slurp, slurp… The comma was now a full stop.

I borrow books from the Grand Library. I read them by the Ocean of Ink.

'How clever, Wow!'

'When we use a comma to separate two independent clauses, it's called comma splicing. Please do not do it. The Grammar Wizard gets upset when she hears it has happened.'

Wow wrote:

These are crispy, tasty commas.

The black printed comma can never be erased.

'Why is there a comma in the first sentence and not in the second one?' asked Wow.

'Well, in the first one, it makes sense to have a comma. The word *crispy* is an adjective for the noun *commas*, and the word *tasty* is also an adjective for the noun *commas*. But, in the second one, something is different. I don't know why.'

'You're right about the first sentence. Both the adjectives, *crispy* and *tasty*, have an equal effect on the noun *commas*. To make sure that they have an equal effect, you can insert the conjunction *and*. *These are crispy* and *tasty commas*.'

'Ah... That's a nice way to check whether the adjectives have the same effect on the noun.'

'Now, for the second sentence... *The black printed comma can never be erased*. Can you add a comma between the adjectives *black* and *printed*?'

'Well...'

Q added a comma. *The black, printed comma can never be erased.*

He said the sentence aloud, adding the conjunction *and* to it. *The black* and *printed comma can never be erased.*

Wow asked, 'What do you think?'

'I still haven't a clue.'

'The two adjectives are linked together. Therefore, they cannot be separated by a comma.'

Q wrote the sentence as it originally was. *The black printed comma can never be erased.*

He read it twice.

'I see what you mean. We're talking about *black printed commas*. The adjectival phrase—*black printed*—describes the comma. We're neither talking about a *black comma* nor about a *printed comma*. We are talking about a *black printed comma*.'

'Exactly... That's enough about commas. There's a pond somewhere close by. It should be over there,' said Wow.

Q tiptoed around the commas drying on the ground. They went around a hill. Shrill voices were shouting words. Sometimes, three different words were screamed at the same time.

Covering his ears, Q went closer to the voices. Six word-peckers were gliding over a pond. Each bird screamed a question word. Why? Where? When? What? Who? How?

'And what are they doing?' asked Q.

'These word-peckers are making question marks. Question marks grow in this pond of black ink. They start out as a dot and a line. When a word-pecker shouts a question word, the dot and the line become larger. Eventually, they form a question mark. This happens after a lot of shouting.'

The word-peckers did not even notice the visitors. The birds were watching their reflections in the ink to make sure they did not crash into each other.

'It looks like a lot of hard work,' said Q.

'It certainly is. These word-peckers have strong lungs.'

'I know we use a question mark at the end of a question. Am I correct?'

'We use a question mark at the end of a direct question. Like the question you just asked me: "*Am I correct?*" Now, when it's an indirect question, don't use a question mark.'

'Can you tell me an indirect question?'

'He asked whether it was correct.'

'Ahhh... An indirect question is when we say a question that was asked by someone else,' said Q.

'Yes. At the end of an indirect question, use a full stop.'

'I've a question. My wife sometimes writes: *Could you buy some handmade paper.* And she ends the sentence with a full stop. Why does she do that? Shouldn't there be a question mark instead?'

The flower in Q's pocket shivered. Wow saw this but did not say anything.

'Your wife is correct. When one writes such a sentence, one is making a polite request. It's a weak command. Your wife expects you to buy some sheets of handmade paper. It really isn't a question. Do you see what I mean?'

'Huh… Now, I do.'

Q saw a line of flowers which looked like tulips. They were in different colours—white, blue, pink, yellow, and purple. The petals sparkled in the sunlight.

'What beautiful flowers!'

'Peek inside one,' said Wow.

Q circled the pond. He peered into a flower's folded petals.

'There's a black dot inside.'

'We use these dots for making punctuation marks: full stops, semicolons, and colons.'

'Can I take one?'

'Yes… Be careful. These dots look a bit delicate. They aren't ready.'

Q gently opened the flower. With his thumb and index finger, he picked up a dot.

'It smells like honey!'

'It tastes like honey too. Somehow, I prefer eating commas, though.'

'How come I never get these smells when I read a book?'

'Haven't you ever put your nose to a page?'

'Never.'

A faint noise came from the dot. When Q held it closer to his ear, he heard the sound: szoomp, szoomp, szoomp.

'All punctuation marks have different smells and sounds,' said Wow.

'I never knew there are all these sounds and smells on a page!'

'A page with punctuation is never dull. Trust me. When do we use a full stop?'

'We use it to mark the end of a sentence. I have a question about dots.'

'Tell me.'

'In some books I have seen three dots in a row. What do they mean?'

'When there are three dots in a row, it is called an ellipsis.'

Q repeated the word in his mind. He liked the sound of it.

He asked, 'What does an ellipsis do?'

'An ellipsis shows that there are missing words from the text of a quotation. Now, go to the board over there.'

'I don't see anything.'

'Just walk straight ahead.'

Q stumbled down a steep slope. He slipped on some stones. Regaining his balance, he went ahead. The bookworm dug all its fifty-two feet into Q's neck. There was the sound of flowing ink. Glugil...Glugil...Glugil... There was no river in sight. Q found it difficult to move his feet. Something was holding them back. He struggled to walk a few more paces forward. His legs were moving in slow motion.

'Wow! What is happening?'

'Stay calm.'

Q stood still. His pants felt heavy and wet.

'You are in the River of Invisible Ink,' Wow said.

'I am in ink!'

'Ink from this river is used to fill the blank space on a page. Blank space is an important part of punctuation.'

'I feel strange,' said Q. 'Can I go back?'

'Walk to the other side of the river.'

Q waded through the invisible ink. After he reached dry land, he squeezed out some ink from his pants.

Wow said, 'As I was saying, blank space is important. We use blank space to divide words, sentences, and paragraphs. Blank space gives order and elegance to a page. Go to the board over there. It was made by the fifth Grammar Wizard.'

On the board was written:

WITHOUTCORRECTPUNCTUATIONTHEREADER
MAYBECONFUSEDASTOWHATTHEWRITERIS
TRYINGTOSAYNEVERTHELESSMANYPEOPLE
DONOTGIVEMUCHTHOUGHTTOPUNCTUA
TIONIFYOUDONOTUSEFULLSTOPSCOMMAS
COLONSANDSEMICOLONSPROPERLYYOUR
WRITINGCOULDBEDIFFICULTTOUNDERSTAND

Wow said, 'Before the time of the fifth Grammar Wizard, all books had pages like this. There was no space between words. There are old books in the Grand Library that are printed like this. I gave up trying to eat words from them. I had to eat all the words in one line in one go. I used to get sick. Tummy ache.'

Q struggled to make sense of these strings of letters.

'The fifth Grammar Wizard felt it would be easier to read when words are separated from one another,' said Wow.

Q flipped through his notebook. His handwriting was neat, but he could have made better use of the blank space on his pages.

'Mmm… I see what you mean,' said Q.

'Could you punctuate the first two sentences?'

Q searched for words in the long strings of letters.

He wrote:

Without correct punctuation, the reader may be confused as to what the writer is trying to say. Nevertheless, many people do not give much thought to punctuation.

He thought for a moment, before writing a very long sentence.

Without correct punctuation, the reader may be confused as to what the writer is trying to say; nevertheless, many people do not give much thought to punctuation.

'Wow, I've used punctuation in two different ways with the same set of words.'

'It's fine.'

'Shouldn't there be just one way. I mean the right way?'

'Well, it depends on your style of writing. As long as you use punctuation correctly, you can punctuate a sentence any way you wish.'

'And I never noticed all this blank space on a page before.'

'I just love being in the space between a chapter heading and the first paragraph. Ahh... There's so much more I want to tell you, but it won't be long before the spell-checker owls start hooting. We can use the bridge over there to cross the river,' said Wow.

'Why didn't I see that bridge before?'

CHAPTER 20

The Punctuation Grove II

It was a narrow bridge made from planks of apostrophe tree wood that were held together by ropes. It rocked sideways as Q walked on it.

Wow said, 'Semicolons. You do know how they look, don't you?'

'A dot above and a comma below.'

'Exactly... Word-peckers make a semicolon by joining a comma with a dot from a flower. Invisible ink sets the comma and dot in place.'

'I'm never sure when to use a semicolon.'

'I'll tell you three ways to use this delightful punctuation mark. First, we use a semicolon to connect two independent clauses. Stop and write this down. *We are spending time at the Punctuation Grove.* Then use a semicolon and write—*I am beginning to appreciate the value of punctuation.*'

They were in the middle of the bridge. Q sat down. After he rolled up his pants till his knees, Q removed his boots and socks. He swivelled around so that his legs went over the side of the bridge. His feet splashed in the flowing invisible ink.

He wrote: *We are spending time at the Punctuation Grove; I am beginning to appreciate the value of punctuation.*

'What do you think?' asked Wow.

'I like that both the independent clauses are related to each other. You used a semicolon when we talked about compound sentences.'

'Yes, I did. Good memory. Now, here is the second way to use a semicolon. We use a semicolon before a conjunctive adverb.'

'What is a conjunctive adverb?'

'A conjunctive adverb establishes a kind of relationship between two independent clauses.'

'Can you give me some examples?'

'Examples of conjunctive adverbs are *furthermore*, *therefore*, and *hence*.'

Q wrote those words down.

Wow said, 'The third Grammar Wizard spoke about the need for good punctuation *semicolon* furthermore, he was the first to cultivate commas.'

'Mmm… The conjunctive adverb links the two independent clauses. Isn't it amazing that he was the first to cultivate commas?' said Q.

'The conjunctive adverb *furthermore* tells us that the second independent clause is more important than the first.'

Q wrote—*I enjoy learning about punctuation; hence I could spend a whole month in the Punctuation Grove.*

Wow asked, 'What kind of relationship does *hence* make?'

Q tapped his pencil on the word *hence*.

'Aha! The first independent clause gives a reason why I could spend a whole month in the Punctuation Grove.'

'Yes. The word *hence* brings out a cause-and-effect relationship between the two independent clauses.'

Q said, 'I really should use more conjunctive adverbs in my writing.'

'Good idea… Now, the third way to use semicolons is when we use them in a list. We may have already used other punctuation marks, but we still want to mark off some sections in the list,' said Wow.

'This I know.'

Q wrote quickly:

Here is the list of people who were at the cottage: Ha, the guardian of the Garden of Grammar; M, the assistant to the Grammar Wizard; Woz, from the Memory Store; and Pil, from the Zero Conditional Zone.

'Excellent. Now, imagine that you replaced all the semicolons with commas. How would it be?'

In his mind, Q replaced all the semicolons with commas:

Here is the list of people who were at the cottage: Ha, the guardian of the Garden of Grammar, M, the assistant to the Grammar Wizard,

Woz, from the Memory Store, and Pil, from the Zero Conditional Zone.

'Mmm… Very confusing,' said Q. 'I don't know whether the phrase—*the guardian of the Garden of Grammar*—refers to Ha or to M. The semicolons divide the list, making everything clear.'

'Exactly… Yes, semicolons and commas go well together. You deserve a comma. Why don't you eat the one we left on the grass to dry?'

They crossed the bridge and found the comma.

'Would you like some?' asked Q.

'No thanks. I've already eaten my quota of commas for the month.'

Q took a bite of his comma. His mouth puckered in delight. The comma had a strong lemony taste.

'We should come back here when we have more time. By the way, do you know how a colon looks?' said Wow.

'A colon has two dots: one above the other. We use it before a list.'

'Show me one.'

Q wrote—*Please bring: a bottle of black ink, two pens and one question mark.*

'Good. We use a colon to introduce a list,' said Wow. 'The second way to use a colon is when we give an explanation.'

Q wrote a sentence. *The word-peckers are frightened: they think Woo will be their boss.*

Wow said, 'Yes. The independent clause—*they think Woo will be their boss*—says why the word-peckers are frightened.'

'What's the third way to use a colon?'

'We use a colon to give more details.'

Q thought for a while before writing this sentence. *My wife is always reading books: she reads three books a week.*

'You are good with colons. Yes, the independent clause—*she reads three books a week*—tells us more about her reading habit,' said Wow.

'Is there any other way to use a colon?'

'Since you like colons so much, I'll tell you a fourth way to use a colon. Write. *Grammar is easy* colon *we make it difficult.*'

Grammar is easy: we make it difficult.

Q read the words slowly. He read the sentence again, this time pausing at the colon. His eyes lit up.

'The two parts of the sentence seem to be saying opposite things. In the first part, we have the word *easy,* and in the second part, we have the word *difficult.* The two independent clauses on either side of the colon are balancing each other.'

'I see you are beginning to appreciate punctuation. You're right. We use a colon to balance or contrast two statements.'

'Most of these sentences are two independent clauses joined by a colon. Does it mean that they are compound sentences?'

'Yes, they are. You are becoming good at grammar.'

'Well, umm… I'm enjoying it. Finally.'

'Let's meet the apostrophe trees.'

On their way back, they saw the black pond where question marks were made. The word-peckers lay on the grass, with their bellies up and their wings spread out. They had finished their work for the day. After screaming question words all day long, the word-peckers were wordless.

Q went to a row of apostrophe trees. Their trunks made pencil-thin shadows on the ground. The black apostrophes glistened in the sunlight.

'Once an apostrophe is fully formed, it detaches from the tree. It floats in the air, but it stays close to its branch. Word-peckers collect the ripe apostrophes,' said Wow.

'But how do these punctuation marks float in the air?'

'It's what apostrophes do. Apostrophes float above a line on a page as well.'

'When do we use apostrophes? I know we use them to show possession.'

'Write the possessive form for these words: *girl, girls, boy, boys,*' said Wow.

Q wrote:

girl's girls'
boy's boys'

'Good… When we want to show possession for a singular noun, the apostrophe comes before the letter *s*. For a plural noun, it comes after the letter *s*. Put me on the page,' said Wow.

The bookworm wrote two phrases:

One weeks time

Two weeks time

Wow said, 'Add apostrophes to these time expressions.'

Q added an apostrophe to each phrase.

One week's time

Two weeks' time

'Exactly. In the first phrase, we're talking about one week. So, the apostrophe comes before the *s*,' said Wow.

'The next phrase has more than one week. It has two weeks. We place the apostrophe after the word—*weeks*.'

'Exactly... Write these two words down: *its* and *its* with an apostrophe after the letter *t*.'

Q wrote *its* and *it's*.

'What is the difference?' asked Wow.

'Well, *its* acts either as a possessive adjective or as a possessive pronoun. While, *it's* is a contraction for *it is*.'

'Exactly... We use an apostrophe to show that a letter or some letters are missing. Don't forget... *It's* can be the short form for *it is* or *it has*. We use the contracted form only in informal speech.'

'We use apostrophes to shorten other words as well. We say: *don't* for *do not*... *I'm* for *I am*... *you're* for *you are*.'

'Exactly... Go to those yellow plants over there.'

The plants looked very much like bamboo shoots.

'We cut these plants to make hyphens and dashes. I have a question for you. Is a hyphen shorter than a dash?' said Wow.

'Mmm... Yes, it is.'

'You're right. When do we use a hyphen?'

'I know we use hyphens with numbers.'

'Exactly. We use hyphens with numbers from twenty-one to ninety-nine.'

Q wrote some words:

twenty-three

seventy-one

one hundred and nine

Wow said, 'You didn't use hyphens with *one hundred and nine.* That's good.'

'Are there any other uses of hyphens?'

'We often use a hyphen when we have a compound adjective.'

'And what's that?'

'A compound adjective is two words that come together to modify a noun. You see, these two words act as a unit. Compound adjectives come in many different forms. I'll tell you about three of them. The first is: adverb + past participle,' said Wow. 'For example, *Ha is a well hyphen known grammarian.*'

Q wrote—*Hu is a well-known grammarian.*

'Ahh... So, *well-known* modifies the noun *grammarian.* I just thought of another compound adjective. Wow is the most *well-read* bookworm I have ever met.'

'Thank you. By the way, how many bookworms do you know?'

'Not many.'

'Hmm... Now, the second form of a compound adjective is: noun + past participle.'

'I love eating *sun-dried* commas.'

'Excellent... The third form is: adjective + present participle.'

'Wow is a *good-looking* bookworm.'

'Mmm… You're giving me lots of compliments today. Now, about dashes… Dashes are used before a list.'

Q wrote: *When you go to Biblios, please buy—two commas, a pencil and a few bookmarks.*

'Exactly. We also use a dash to mark out a word or a group of words,' said Wow.

While he was thinking of what to write, Q doodled on a yellow page. He then wrote a long sentence.

The Grand Librarian—who knows grammar so well—must understand that this is not the way to become the Grammar Wizard.

'Yes, I'm as surprised as you are about K,' said Wow. 'See how the group of words marked out by the dashes stands out from the rest of the sentence.'

'When will the spell-checker owls start hooting?'

'We've just enough time to talk about exclamation marks. Hurry to those hedges over there.'

The hedges formed a triangle. There was a gap in one of its sides. Q squeezed through it.

'You should be sitting down for this,' said Wow.

'Why?'

'I'm going to tell you how exclamation marks are made.'

Q sat down, folding one leg. He stretched the other leg out onto the grass. The hedges were dense with leaves and twigs. He saw that many twigs were broken.

'An exclamation mark can come at the end of a sentence that has a lot of emotion. An exclamation mark can come after an interjection. An exclamation mark can also come after a command. For example: Stop! Now, it's hard to make an exclamation mark. The person in this triangle must be surprised or shocked,' said Wow.

'Huh... And then what happens?'

'They drop from the sky; no one knows why.'

'It's impossible. Wow, you're pulling my leg.'

'I thought you'd say that. Just to prove to you it works, I'll say something that will surprise you.'

The bookworm slid down Q's back and landed on the ground. It hid under the hedges.

'Can you hear me?' Wow yelled.

'Yes.'

'Your wife works with the Grammar Wizard. N is M.'

'N is the assistant to the Grammar Wizard!'

'Wait, there's more. She is now a grammatica flower. N is in your pocket.'

Q put his hands on his heart.

'What!'

He did not hear the whistling sound coming from above. Two exclamation marks hit him. Thump! Thump!

'Ouch!'

The exclamation marks bounced off his head. A third exclamation mark was falling. But this time, Q heard it. He rolled away just in time to avoid it.

The bookworm cautiously walked out from under the hedges. It climbed onto the long part of an exclamation mark.

'You could've warned me that the exclamation marks will hit me,' said Q, massaging the two bumps on his head.

'Look at it this way... You'll never forget how exclamation marks are made. By the way, we also use exclamation marks after sounds. Your sound was: thump!'

Q cupped his hand over his left ear, anxiously listening for any whistling sounds.

'Some advice... When you write, don't use too many exclamation marks. As you now know, they are quite difficult to make. They lose their impact when you use too many of them. Use them only when you really have to,' said Wow.

Q held the flower in his hands.

'Is this really my wife?'

'It is.'

Q caressed the stem of the flower.

'N… Can you hear me? Is it really you? Are you okay?'

There was a long silence. And then the spell-checker owls hooted:

hoo HOO hoo HOO hoo HOO hoo HOO hoo HOO

CHAPTER 21

Thirteen Questions

'I found K's boat. It was on the River of Black Ink,' said Ha.
'K would've come to the Garden of Grammar by the River of Green Ink. How come his boat ended up here?' said P.

'He must have dragged it to the River of Black Ink and let it float away.'

'So that we would spend all our time searching for the Grammar Wizard in this part of the Dimension. Well, well… K has been planning this for some time.'

Q and Wow returned as the hoots from the spell-checker owls were fading.

'You should leave tomorrow early morning. If you travel by balloon, you'll reach the cottage before evening,' P said to Q.

'We will use K's boat to reach the garden. It has three propellers. We will get there in good time,' said Ha.

'Am I really ready for this? I mean, what happens if I don't know the answers to K's questions?' Q asked.

'Do you remember the ceiling of the main reading hall at the Grand Library?' Wow asked.

'How could I forget? Those grammarians were painting, playing football, and cooking.'

'They were living life. They were curious about everything. They were not teaching grammar to anyone,' said Wow.

'What are you trying to tell me?' asked Q, scratching his head.

Wow, curled up near the balloon, was already asleep.

'Give us your final answer tomorrow morning,' said Ha.

Q slept against an apostrophe tree. He dreamt of a world where the magic trees would not speak in the breeze. And where the Word Fields would be empty and quiet. And where the people of Biblios would be fighting with each other, all the time.

As the sun rose, the shadow of an apostrophe crept across his face. He woke up when he heard a whirring sound. P was testing the propellers of the balloon.

Q stood up and stretched his arms. Above him were a bunch of floating apostrophes. A breeze came, making the apostrophes gently bump into each other. Q knew what he had to do.

'I will go to the garden.'

'Have some commas,' said Wow.

'Drink the rest of the grammar potion,' said P. 'It'll help you remember everything'.

Q ate two crisp commas. As he sipped the grammar potion, he wondered whether it would give him enough strength to face the Grand Librarian of Biblios.

P called him over to the balloon. Above the basket, there were three cylinders containing energy articles. They powered the flame which heated the air in the balloon.

'There are air currents above us. You must keep rising until you find an air current flowing to where you want to go to. If you need to go up, raise this lever. It'll increase the strength of the flame. Use the propellers to descend,' said P.

Q nodded his head. He had seen P operate the balloon many times by now.

P went on: 'Use the propellers to steer you in a particular direction. If the wind is very strong, they may not be effective, though. To reach the Garden of Grammar, all you have to do is follow the River of Black Ink.'

As the balloon rose, it brushed against the branches of an apostrophe tree. Q reached out to touch an apostrophe. It felt spongy. He saw that the word-peckers were busy flying over the pond, shouting question words. A thick line curved through the Punctuation Grove. He guessed that the line was the River of Invisible Ink. The balloon was drifting away from the river he was supposed to follow. Q increased the strength of the flame. He found a strong air current flowing east.

Sitting cross-legged, he took out the flower and stroked a petal.

'Stop daydreaming,' said a voice. 'Read all the notes you've made. We'll be there before you know it.'

'N!' shouted Q.

'I'm using telepathy to communicate with you.'

'But... But... How did you become a flower?'

'I'll tell you later. Read your notes. Please!'

Q opened his notebook. He started with his notes on articles. He read about the parts of speech and the present tense, past tense, and future time. Down below, the word-peckers cooed: the balloon was flying over the Word Fields.

'I feel there's something you aren't telling me,' he said, while he was on the page that had notes on the second conditional.

'Don't talk.'

After reading about punctuation, he stood up to shake his left leg. It had fallen asleep. The snow-capped peaks of the Dimension Mountain Range were now in sight.

The balloon landed in the garden. The grammatica flowers drooped to the ground. Q walked cautiously, as if he had never been there before. When he passed the flowers, they tried to straighten themselves. Some opened their petals, but only for a few seconds. A word-pecker was flying, lazily flapping its wings. It was heading towards the cottage.

'It's Woo,' mumbled Q.

'Beware of that word-pecker,' said the flower in Q's pocket.

When Q saw the white walls of the cottage, K opened the door. He swaggered out, wearing a shimmering purple robe. A tall, pointy hat was on his head. He smirked before returning inside. The door was left ajar.

Q thought: *He looks like a grammar wizard alright, but not a friendly one.*

'Go to him,' said the flower. 'We need to find out what he wants.'.

Q hesitantly entered the cottage. The Grammar Wizard was tied to a chair. She could barely move her arms and legs.

She whispered, 'I knew you would come.'

'Do you know why you are here, Q?' asked K.

'We saw the word clouds you sent us.'

'There is much more to it than that,' said K. 'Sit down.'

He noticed the blue flower in Q's coat pocket.

'That is no ordinary grammatica flower,' K said.

'A very ordinary flower. Tell me what you want.'

'Ah, you are becoming confident. Interesting.'

Woo glided into the room through an open window.

K continued: 'The Grammar Wizard has agreed to appoint me as the next Grammar Wizard. However, for some reason, all the spell-checker owls think that you are the one who is destined to save the Dimension. Ha! Whoever it is, it most certainly is not you. As the owls feel so strongly about this, I have come to an agreement with them. You will be asked thirteen questions. If you answer more than two questions incorrectly, I become the new Grammar Wizard. However, if you answer at least eleven questions correctly, I agree to return to the Grand Library. Simple. Is it clear?'

'I had no choice. K threatened to pour anti-grammatical sand over the entire garden,' said the Grammar Wizard.

'After I become the Grammar Wizard, I might just throw some sand on a few flowers, just to see what happens,' said K.

The Grammar Wizard struggled wildly. She shook her head so much that her spectacles slid down to the tip of her nose.

'Let her go,' said Q.

'I shall release her after you answer the last question. You have my word. Do you accept the challenge?' said K.

'I do.'

Woo glared at the flower tucked in Q's breast pocket.

K asked, 'Have you really come alone? As I instructed you to.'

Q did not answer the question.

'What are you doing?' said the flower to Q. 'Say yes.'

'I am not alone,' said Q.

'Aha! Just as I suspected… It is M. I was wondering where she disappeared to. The flowers must have cast a spell on her,' said K.

'I'll leave it here,' said Q. 'And I'll take it when I leave.'

He placed the flower on the table.

Woo hopped up to its stem, and cooed, 'Wrr… Wrr…'

'Good work, Woo. We finally found her,' said K. 'Let us finish this, once and for all. My dear Grammar Wizard please wait here, if you don't mind, that is. Once your grammarian has answered more than two questions incorrectly, the lamp will be mine. You shall be free to go home.'

K and Q stood near the River of Red Ink. On the other side of the river, three spell-checker owls perched on a branch of an oak tree. In the tree, there was a hole. And in the hole, there was a scroll.

'I want to get this over and done with. Don't look so worried. Soon you will be with your precious flower. Q of Alphabet village… Are you ready for the first question?' asked K.

'Yes.'

The three spell-checker owls nodded to each other. Clutching the edge of the scroll in its beak, an owl pulled the scroll out of the tree. After flying to the other side of the river, the owl let go of the scroll when it was above K's eager hands.

'The thirteen questions… These were prepared by a committee of spell-checker owls. I had nothing to do with it. Nothing at all,' said K.

He broke the red seal and unfurled the scroll.

'The first question is about the zero article. Is this correct? *We believe in peace.*'

Woo hovered above K. In its beak was the special grammatica flower. The word-pecker bit hard into the flower's stem.

Q cried out, 'No!'

'This is going to be easier than I thought,' said K to himself.

'I didn't mean that the sentence was wrong. It is correct. We use the zero article before the abstract noun *peace* because we are talking about *peace* in general.'

K scratched his chin.

'Too late. Your first answer is always the final answer. The spell-checker owls have already recorded it.'

'Tell Woo to stop hurting the flower,' said Q.

'As you wish. Woo, leave the flower alone.'

Woo dropped it over a bed of black grammatica flowers. With great effort, these flowers opened their petals to cushion the fall of the flower.

'May we carry on?' asked K.

'Yes.'

'For the first question, you gave me an incorrect answer.'

'I didn't even answer it.'

'Question number two. What is the difference between the past simple and the past perfect?'

'I... I don't know.'

'Ha ha... I knew you know nothing of grammar. Go back to school.'

'Please, free the Grammar Wizard... What has she done to you?'

'Wrong answer!'

'Answer the next question for me,' said the flower to Q.

'What is the difference between these two sentences? *I will rule the Grammar Dimension. I am going to rule the Grammar Dimension.*'

'In the first sentence, you are deciding right now that you want to rule the Dimension. In the second sentence, you have already decided in the past that you want to rule the Dimension, and you are telling me about it right now.'

The three spell-checker owls hooted: 'Hoo! Hoo!'

'Hmm... Your answer is correct. Next question. Is this correct? *Before midnight, I will become the Grammar Wizard.*'

'It's wrong. It should be in the form of the future perfect tense. *Before midnight, I will have become the Grammar Wizard.*'

'Are you sure?' asked K.

'Yes.'

'Hoo! Hoo!'

'Correct again... *I have been to the Word Fields yesterday morning.* Is it correct?'

'It's wrong. We can't use finished time, *yesterday morning*, with the present perfect. Whenever we use the present perfect, it has to be *unfinished time.*'

'Hoo! Hoo!'

Q felt the effects of Grammar Potion Number 9. He was also encouraged by the hooting from the spell-checker owls.

'*I hate waiting.* Is the word *waiting* a gerund?'

'In that sentence, the word *waiting* acts like a noun. It's a gerund.'

'Hoo! Hoo!'

K was getting worried. *What is happening? When I met Q at the Grand Library, he was not even sure how to use the present simple tense. Let me see whether he can answer the next question.*

'Identify this type of sentence. *You have learnt a lot of grammar, but it is my destiny to become the Grammar Wizard.*'

'Both the clauses are independent clauses, and they are joined by a co-ordinating conjunction. It has to be a compound sentence.'

'Hoo! Hoo!'

'Woo! You said Q does not know any grammar. How is he answering all these questions?' said K.

'Maybe the grammatica flower are helping him.'

K glared at the blue flower that was on the grass.

'Of course. That must be it. M must have been telling him the answers. Throw the flower into the river. At once!'

After snatching the flower from the ground, Woo flung it into the fast-flowing red ink.

'Listen to me very carefully. I know the flower is your wife. If you answer one more question incorrectly, I will tell Woo to bring her back,' said K. 'Decide now. It is important you tell me right now. Look at the river. See how fast the ink flows. Once she is in the Ocean of Ink, it will be too late. She will be lost, forever.'

Q saw the blue flower in the red ink. The river's strong current pressed the flower against a stone. Then the flower was swept away, moving fast—away from Q.

He hoped his friends would arrive in time to save N.

'Ask your question,' said Q, gritting his teeth.

'Identify which conditional this is in. *If you were me, you would want the Lamp of Grammar.*'

'It's in the second conditional. And, I would never want to be you.'

'Hoo! Hoo!'

'Why are you being so unreasonable? All you have to do is answer one question incorrectly. Woo will rescue your wife.'

'The next question.'

'Is the use of punctuation correct? *Invisible ink is as important as words on a page* semicolon *because the invisible ink keeps the words in place.*'

'It's wrong. A semicolon links two independent clauses. In your sentence, the second clause is a dependent clause.'

'Hoo! Hoo!'

'*If I had studied harder at grammar school, I could have become the Grammar Wizard years ago.* Identify which conditional it is in.'

'The third conditional.'

'Hoo! Hoo!'

K glanced at the spell-checker owls. They were keeping score of all the correct and incorrect answers. He knew that he could not influence them. Spell-checker owls were honest birds.

Leaning into Q, K whispered, 'When I become the Grammar Wizard, I can give you whatever you want. Books. Power. Do you want to be the Grand Librarian? Just tell me what you want!'

Q did not say a word. K's lip curled as he read the next question.

'Identify the type of dependent clause in this sentence. *I am the man that will change the Grammar Dimension forever.*'

'It contains a relative clause: *that will change the Grammar Dimension forever.*'

'Hoo! Hoo!'

'Is this correct? *The quality of the quill pens are excellent.*'

'The quality of the quill pens *is* excellent. The subject of the sentence is *quality*. The noun *pens* is part of the prepositional phrase.'

'Hoo! Hoo!'

K thrust his hand into his robe. He brought out a saltshaker and placed it on the ground.

'Do you see this? It is filled with anti-grammatical sand. If you answer the next question correctly, I shall tell Woo to sprinkle ALL this anti-grammatical sand ALL over your precious grammatica flowers. They will die. DIE! When the flowers die, the Garden of Grammar will be no more. Q, it will be ALL your fault.'

'Ask the last question.'

K held the scroll up to read the thirteenth question. A smile spread across his thin face. *Even if Q wants to answer this question, he will not be able to. How could someone like him, who has no real understanding of grammar, answer such a profound question? I am certain Wow and P have not prepared him for this kind of question. After all these years of unhappiness, the Lamp of Grammar is mine. Finally.*

He lowered the scroll. His eyes sparkled. With a smirk on his face, he asked the last question.

'What is grammar?'

The three owls on the other side of the river strained their ears. They did not want to miss a single syllable. The owl in the middle covered its eyes with its wings.

Q's shoulders drooped when he heard the last question. He did not have an answer for it. He did not have a clue. He glanced at the delicate flowers around him. *If K throws anti-grammatical sand on them, they will surely die. If they die, the Garden of Grammar will be destroyed. The Grammar Dimension will fall back into chaos. All because of me...*

He was about to tell K that he did not know the answer. He was about to beg him to free the Grammar Wizard. He was about to plead with him not to use anti-grammatical sand.

A flash of light came from the grass. Q squinted at a bunch of green grammatica flowers. His eyes were filled with joy. Wow's golden spectacles were reflecting sunlight. Q's friends had finally arrived!

Closing his eyes, Q thought about the question. *What is grammar? He remembered what Woz told him at the Memory Store: when all else fails, memory can save you. And so, Q recalled all that he had seen and done during his travels across the Dimension. He could taste the apple from the Circle of Magic Trees. He recollected the eight parts of speech. He heard the deafening sound of thunder over the Articles Station, and he recollected how some words go with 'a' and how some other words go with 'an'. He saw Woz's bald head reflecting candlelight in the Memory Store, and he thought about the past continuous tense. Swimming in the cold, salty ink of the Sea of Wishes... Sliding into the Third Conditional Zone... Meeting the Uncountables... Ha telling him about the future time... At the Memory Store, in his grammar dream, even in the Conditional Zones... The words always followed a pattern. There was a structure... He thought about the word-peckers in the Word Fields, and what Wow told him about clauses and phrases. Again, there was always a reason why each word was in its place in a sentence.*

K's eyelids were half closed, as he waited patiently for an incorrect answer. His hands formed a pyramid, with his fingertips lightly pressing against each other. He was already behaving as if he were the Grammar Wizard.

'Grammar shows the relationship between words,' said Q.

'Hoo! Hoo! Hoo! Hoo!'

'How could you know that? When I met you, you knew nothing of grammar.'

K clenched his teeth. He glanced at the saltshaker near his feet.

'Woo... Sprinkle this sand over the flowers. If I cannot have the lamp, then no one else can!'

Clutching the saltshaker, the word-pecker flapped about. It swooped down over a bed of terrified grammatica flowers.

'Ha, ha, ha,' K laughed out loud.

Just as Woo was about to tilt the small holes of the saltshaker downwards, a hairy hand grabbed its beak. Another hairy hand grabbed the saltshaker.

'Did someone call me?' asked Ha.

'Where did you come from? Bah... I should've covered you in sand,' said K.

Turning around, the Grand Librarian dashed towards the cottage. He still had some anti-grammatical sand with him. He could use it to hold the Grammar Wizard hostage. While he was running, he took out his pair of gloves. He managed to put one on, but the other one fell to the ground. He did not stop to pick it up.

K kicked the door open. The rope lay in a bundle on the floor.

The Grammar Wizard, with her arms crossed, stood behind the chair.

'P, arrest the Grand Librarian of Biblios.'

P picked up the rope.

'K, it's over.'

With his gloved hand, the Grand Librarian took out some sand from his pouch. Spellbound by the silvery sand, P dropped the rope.

'Why are you doing this?' asked the Grammar Wizard.

'The Grammar Council just talks and talks and talks. Someone needs to take charge and make decisions on the future of grammar.'

K raised his arm to hurl the sand at them.

'Once this is over, you'll understand why I had to do this.'

K swung his forearm forward. P jumped in front of the Grammar Wizard.

'There is no place for your sand in my garden,' said Ha, who was in the doorway.

Leaping up, Ha grabbed K's raised wrist. K pushed Ha back. When K did so, some sand fell onto his forehead. K's eyes widened in horror. As he tried desperately to remove the sand from his face, he crumpled to the floor.

Ha, the guardian of the Garden of Grammar, did not move. There was still some anti-grammatical sand in K's hand. And there was more sand in K's pouch, which was now on the floor. Ha rushed outside and returned wearing K's other glove. He took the sand from K's hand and put it in the pouch. He tied the pouch. Everyone sighed in relief.

'What should we do with all this anti-grammatical sand?' asked Ha.

'There is a spell to reverse it. It is in *The Grammar of Spells*,' said the Grammar Wizard.

'Wow knows where the book is,' said P.

'Will K lose his knowledge of grammar?' asked the Grammar Wizard.

'Not at all. Just a few grains of sand touched him,' said Ha.

'I would like to have a chat with him after he wakes up,' said the Grammar Wizard.

In the garden, Q was on his hands and knees.

'Wow, where are you?'

'I'm right here on your shoulder. I just spoke with the spell-checker owls. They said you answered the questions brilliantly. As for K's last question, I crossed all my legs. I fell down!'

'My wife, N… The grammatica flower… She's in the river.'

'Let's hurry.'

The balloon flew over the restless river. When he looked at the horizon, Q saw a cliff. From this cliff, the River of Red Ink plunged into the ocean. The roar of the ink crashing into the ocean sent shivers down his spine.

The balloon landed with a thud. He tumbled out of the basket. His eyes searched the raging ink. There was no sign of a flower.

At the edge of the cliff, there were three people. They gazed at the Ocean of Ink. In this part of the ocean, all the ink was red. The sun lit up the thin, red clouds that were on the horizon.

Q recognized the three people who were talking with one another.

Running towards them, he shouted, 'I did it! I did it!'

A lady with a pencil in her hair turned around. It was Maz. The other two people turned around as well. They were Woz and the

Leader of the Uncountables. Everyone had dark circles under their eyes.

Tears of joy streamed down their cheeks. The Leader of the Uncountables always had three grey silk handkerchiefs. He gave one to Woz and one to Maz.

Q was out of breath when he reached them.

'We were standing here, not knowing what to do. We are so proud of you,' said Maz.

Q said, 'Woz! Thank you for telling me about the importance of memory. Your words saved me.'

'Well, I'm overjoyed that you umm... remembered!' said Woz.

'I could never have done this without all of you. You believed in me, even when...,' said Q.

'Stay with us to watch the sunset,' said the Leader of the Uncountables.

Q wiped the tears from his cheeks.

'I'm searching for a flower. I...I fear it is already in the ocean. I don't know...'

'A grammatica flower called out to me. I do not know how, or why, but it did,' said Maz.

'We managed to catch it before it fell into the ocean,' said Woz.

Maz was holding a basket. In it was a blue flower.

'It is my wife,' said Q.

'The flower is in pain. The Grammar Wizard will know what to do,' said the Leader of the Uncountables. 'Leave immediately.'

Q and Wow left with the flower. Maz, Woz, and the Leader of the Uncountables waved at the balloon as it rose into the air.

Woz said, 'After you finish crying, give me your handkerchiefs. I never want to forget this moment.'

'Oh Woz,' said Maz. 'You and your memory jars!'

The balloon landed near the cottage. The door was wide open. The Grammar Wizard was in her rocking chair, while P and Ha sat on the orange sofa. Ha held Woo, the word-pecker, tightly. Woo looked glum.

Q, with trembling hands, kneeled before the Grammar Wizard.

'Please, please help me! N is a grammatica flower.'

'Place the flower on the carpet.'

The Grammar Wizard chanted a spell:

In the name of all grammatical creatures, and the Garden of Grammar;

In the name of all the four rivers of visible ink, and the Dimension Mountain Range;

In the name of all the eight parts of speech, and the Circle of Magic Trees;

In the name of the Second Conditional, and all things unreal;

Restore this person to her original form!

Poof! N was before them. She smiled weakly, but her legs had no strength. Q caught her as she fell. He sprinkled some cold, black ink on her face.

N mumbled, 'Foo... Foo... Food.'

The Grammar Wizard went into the kitchen and heated a pan. She fried a comma in it. She flipped the comma in the pan. The comma was cooked in a minute. After eating the comma and drinking a mixture of warm green and black ink, N felt much better.

Q told them how he had answered the thirteenth question. P said he was so happy that he had taken Q to all the four corners of the Dimension. They were all relieved that everything ended well.

The Grammar Wizard went to the bookshelf to take the lamp. She placed it on the round table. The soft light from the lamp lit her kind, intelligent face. It was the first time Q noticed the Lamp of Grammar.

'I have something to say. I am planning to retire,' said the Grammar Wizard.

'Why?' Ha asked.

'I want to spend more time with my husband,' she replied.

After removing her spectacles, she folded them and placed them beside the lamp. Grinning at P, she carefully removed her wig. P wondered what the Grammar Wizard was doing. She peeled off the dot on her chin.

'Now, do you recognise me?'

'How is this... possible?' mumbled P.

'You men are so easy to fool,' said X, the Grammar Wizard, with a wink.

'You raise your eyebrow... just like X... How could it... You are the...'

P had served the Grammar Wizard for two decades. He needed some time to get over this shock.

'As I was saying,' said the Grammar Wizard, 'I am planning to retire soon. I have spoken with the magic trees. They are preparing questions for a competition that is open to all. The winner will be presented with this lamp. She or he will be the next Grammar Wizard.'

'How can I take part in the competition? Ah... Before that, I need to go to the Third Conditional Zone to get some more Grammar Potion Number 9,' said Q.

'Your grammar potion has no magic in it whatsoever. It's pomegranate juice,' said the Grammar Wizard.

'But I saw the secret ingredient,' said Q.

'The secret ingredient is a mixture of cinnamon and sugar,' said N.

'And what about those green ice cubes which floated in the air?' asked Q.

'There must have been invisible ink in the bowl,' replied P, with a shrug.

Everyone, except Q, laughed.

'How could you not tell me? Well, come to think of it, it was probably better I didn't know the truth. Anyways, I still want to be the next Grammar Wizard,' said Q.

'Darling, you've done so much already,' said N. 'Let me become the Grammar Wizard, and you can be my assistant.'

'That does seem to be the pattern,' said P, still looking a bit lost.

'What do you have to say about all this, Wow?' asked Q.

The bookworm was busy making notes on a sheet of paper.

'What are you doing?' asked N.

'I'm writing a book on how Q saved the garden. The story will be full of excitement and grammar,' replied Wow.

'Have you thought of a title yet?' asked N.

'I'm finding it difficult to come up with a one. The title should somehow sum up all that Q has seen... All that we have done... All that we have gone through,' said Wow.

Smiling, N snapped her fingers.

'I might just have a title for you.'

'What would that be?' asked the Grammar Wizard, raising an eyebrow.

P, Q, and Ha leaned forward. Even Woo looked up. Wow waited on a page.

N whispered, 'Q in the Garden of Grammar.'

Bibliography

Carey, G.V. (1978). *Mind the Stop*. London, UK: Penguin Books.

Clark, Roy Peter (2010). *The Glamour of Grammar*. New York, USA: Little, Brown and Company.

Murphy, R. (1994). *Intermediate English Grammar* (Second Edition). New Delhi, India: Cambridge University Press.

Sacks, David (2003). *Letter Perfect*. New York, USA: Broadway Books.

Swan M. (2010). *Practical English Usage* (Third Edition). New Delhi, India: Oxford University Press.

Online resources

BBC Learning English, bbc.co.uk/learningenglish/

British Council Learn English, learnenglish.britishcouncil.org

Cambridge Dictionaries Online, dictionary.cambridge.org

ThoughtCo., https://www.thoughtco.com/esl-grammar-4133089

About the Author

Amal Fabian started his teaching career with the British Council in India.

He has taught adults as well as teenagers at the British Council, Chennai.

In Delhi, as a corporate trainer for the British Council, he has delivered training sessions on presentation skills, report writing, e-mail writing, pronunciation, and grammar at MNCs, Indian companies, and colleges.

He has also conducted *Train the Trainer* programmes. And he has been an IELTS examiner for both speaking and writing.

As an online teacher with the British Council, he has taught students from countries such as Colombia, Mexico, Saudi Arabia, Malaysia, Japan, Ukraine, and France.

In the morning, when he has time, he makes pancakes. He enjoys swimming. He is a self-confessed bookworm who would like to spend all his time reading, if he could.

His blog on English language learning is www.amalfabian.com.